The Seed of the Sacred Fig

1. INT. PROSECUTOR'S OFFICE- DAY

CLOSE SHOT:

A hand places eight bullets of a handgun on the table, one by one.

(O.S.) MAN

Take one, two, three, four, five, six, seven, eight...

Iman's hands enter the frame and take the bullets. Then the man's hand places a form on the table: a receipt for the gun. He underlines a number and leaves the pen on the paper.

MAN

this is its serial number... check it and then sign...

After a pause, Iman's hand enters the frame. He is holding his own pen and signs with it.

2. INT. LATER, COURTHOUSE, SUBMISSION CORRIDOR- DAY

Both sides of the narrow, long, and gloomy corridor are decorated with life-size pictures of generals and military casualties in standing positions. In all the pictures, their hands are laid on their chest as a sign of submission. Through these images, Iman walks toward the camera.

3. INT./EXT. TEHRAN'S STREETS TO IMAMZADEH- DAY/NIGHT (EVENING TO MIDNIGHT), IMAN'S CAR

Iman is driving. You can see joy and pride on his face. His car is speeding through the highway that is surrounded by tall sound barrier walls. At an intersection, he stops at a red light. Looking around proudly, he glances at the gun on the chair next to him.

He passes through the highway (Sadr highway, with bridge foundations), the side road (Fasham mountain that can be seen on the road), and the dirt road. He reaches the mountains at midnight. He parks the car, takes off his shoes, and walks up the steps on the mountainside, barefoot. Facing Imamzadeh's shrine, he places his hand on his chest. Inside the shrine, he starts praying and rubs his forehead on the ground.

(XLS) in the moonlight, on a desert road, Iman's car drives back.

(Film's title) SEED OF THE SACRED TREE

4. INT. IMAN AND NAJMEH'S APT - DAWN

Bathroom. Iman is taking a shower.

Kitchen. Najmeh prepares breakfast and puts it on a tray. Pours the tea and takes the tray to the bedroom. One can feel the warmth of family life.

bedroom. Najmeh enters with a tray. Iman is drying his hair while wearing towels. Najmeh puts the tray on top of the drawer next to Iman.

>   IMAN
>
>   Thanks.

Seeing Iman's messy eyebrows, Najmeh fixes them with her thumb.

>   NAJMEH
>
>   Congratulations. Your prayers have been answered…

Iman nods in gratitude. He picks up the teacup from the tray and sits on the edge of the bed.

>   NAJMEH
>
> May God rest his soul; I wish your father was here with us to
>   see this.

Iman drinks his tea. He says under his breath *"May God rest his soul"*.

>   NAJMEH
>
> I am very happy, for the girls. Finally, our financial situation
>   will improve. Hopefully, they will give us a three-bedroom

house. They are all grown up now, it's difficult for them to share a room.

IMAN

It will take several months.

NAJMEH

It doesn't matter.

Iman takes the gun out of the drawer and shows it to Najmeh. Najmeh is taken aback and looks at it with fear.

IMAN

Don't be afraid, they gave it to me for personal protection.

Najmeh contemplates for a moment.

IMAN

try it...

NAJMEH

No, I don't like to, it's dangerous.

IMAN

Take it.

Najmeh holds the gun for a moment. Iman laughs. It's as if he's enjoying himself unconsciously. Najmeh returns the gun. Iman puts it back in the drawer.

NAJMEH

I think it's time to talk about your job with the girls.

IMAN

Not yet...

NAMJMEH

Why? It's a very good opportunity. You're a judge now! If the kids know, they will be proud of you.

IMAN

Not a judge, an investigating judge.

NAJMEH

Whatever. Soon you'll become an advisory judge and then a chief judge, right? Won't you?

Iman nods in approval.

NAJMEH

Well, then the girls need to know these things. It affects their behavior. They're young, they must be more considerate because of your job.

IMAN

You know the situation is different for revolutionary courts, people don't have a positive perception.

NAJMEH

Yes, but we cannot hide it from the kids forever. You always waited for an opportunity to talk to them about your job. Now is your chance.

Iman takes a moment to think it over.

NAJMEH

Tonight, four of us will go to a restaurant. We'll have a little celebration for your promotion, and then we'll have a conversation as well and share some things with the kids.

IMAN

How much can we share?

NAJMEH

Leave it to me.

Iman seems to be content with this plan and continues drinking his tea.

5. INT. IMAN AND NAJMEH'S APT. KITCHEN -DAY

By the kitchen's island, Sana is putting the plates and breakfast items on the table, one by one. Rezvan is preparing fried eggs, and Najmeh is pouring tea for everyone. From time to time, the clanking of dishes while being placed on the table, can be heard in the background.

NAJMEH

Sana, keep it down dear, your dad is sleeping.

Sana does not answer.

REZVAN

But what would happen if I'm not there?

NAJMEH

What do you mean by not being there? I said it's an important conversation, four of us should be there!

Najmeh takes the tray and goes toward the table. Then she starts putting the cups next to the plates.

REZVAN

Well, tell me now.

NAJMEH

You don't seem to understand what I'm saying. Your dad should be there, it is both a celebration and some sort of family meeting.

REZVAN

Celebration for what?

Najmeh sits behind the table.

NAJMEH

You'll find out tonight.

Putting the pan with fried eggs on the table, Rezvan takes a seat.

REZVAN

Mom, please don't ruin my night, Sadaf is coming back from her town. In fact, she is coming earlier because of tonight's plan. I asked her to come earlier, how does it look like if I don't show up myself?

NAJMEH

My darling, this is an exceptional night, you and your friends can go to the cafe another day.

REZVAN

What do you mean another day? We made plans ten days ago; I can't just switch things up now. There are too many people involved.

NAJMEH

Rezvan, your family should be your priority.

The sound of moving the chair draws the attention.

NAJMEH

Sana, dear, didn't I say Dad is sleeping?

Sana glances at her mother and then sits at the table.

SANA

I got it. what happened now that we are going to have a celebration and a meeting at the same time?

NAJMEH

I can only say it's good news. In all these twenty-two years with your father, I was waiting for a day like this.

Sana nods.

REZVAN

Mom, you're killing us! Just tell us what it is!

NAJMEH

Tonight, at the restaurant.

6. INT./EXT. GARDEN RESTAURANT - Night

Restaurant's yard.

In the outdoor area of a traditional garden restaurant, a few gazebos are arranged in a row not too far from each other. The gazebos are covered with semi-transparent curtains. The sound of traditional Iranian music can be heard. The waiters come and go between the gazebos with trays of food in their hands.

In gazebo.

Sana, Rezvan, Najmeh, and Iman are sitting around a table and eating.

IMAN

When a case is presented in court, there should be investigations to collect correct and complete data. The collection of this information is the responsibility of several specialists who are trusted by the judicial system. These people must remain anonymous.

REZVAN

Why?

IMAN

Because they are at risk, both themselves and their families.

REZVAN

what risk?

IMAN

Most cases have a winner and a loser. The loser might think that they've become a victim of interpersonal conflicts, partiality, or anything unfair during the process of their case. Then they may decide to take revenge.

SANA

Well, the risks persist even now that you've become a judge. What made you decide to share the truth?

                              IMAN

First of all, it is better to say an investigating judge. The
investigating judge is the first judge of the case. Second, we
   decided to tell you because you've grown up now. You can
understand the situation and act responsibly and appropriately.

                             NAJMEH

 There are also things that you should be careful about, more
        than before. As it may impact your Dad negatively.

                              SANA

                           like what?

                             NAJMEH

For example, your hijab. Like the photos, you post on Instagram.
 Most of the social behavior that others see. Some people might
          see and report them. It will be bad for Dad.

                             REZVAN

                We only hang out with Dad's friends.

                             NAJMEH

                 I'm talking exactly about them.

                              SANA

What does my Instagram have to do with Dad? also, one can use
                 Instagram with a fake account.

                             NAJMEH

   That's what I'm talking about. You should know how to act
properly. You should know where to go, who to hang out with,
             what to wear, what to say or not to say.

7. INT. APT. GIRLS' ROOM - NIGHT

The girls' bedroom is rather small, with a bunk bed, a small
desk, and a closet. Sana and Rezvan are lying in their beds.
Sana in the top bunk, is lying down in reverse so that she speak
with Rezvan face to face.

SANA

Look, every year on the first day of school, teachers ask what is your father's job? I used to say an employee until now. What should I say when schools start on Saturday?

REZVAN

Just like before, you have to say an employee.

SANA

No way genius...so what's the difference now?

REZVAN

There's no difference. just that before you weren't responsible for protecting information, now you are.

SANA

Why bother telling us then?

REZVAN

You don't care if your father is an important person?

SANA

No

REZVAN

Seriously?

SANA

What does my father's job have to do with me?

REZVAN

are you messing with me right now?

SANA

No, honestly. It really doesn't matter.

                        REZVAN

   I mean, wouldn't you care if Dad was selling cigarettes in the
                        streets right now?

                         SANA

                 Is it important to you?

                        REZVAN

                 Of course, it's important.

Sana shrugs her shoulders and lies down.

8. INT. PROSECUTOR'S OFFICE, SUBMISSION CORRIDOR- DAY

With a paper in his hand, Iman passes through the submission
corridor and enters Qaderi's office.

                         IMAN

                      what is this?

Iman passes the paper to Qaderi. After reading the text, Qaderi
pauses a moment.

                        QADERI

                       It's clear…

                         IMAN

              But I haven't read the file yet.

                        QADERI

   Whether you read it or not, you must write the sentence and sign
                 it. It's the prosecutor's order.

Iman anxiously looks at Qaderi.

                         IMAN

              I can't do that; I swore for justice!

Shocked and speechless, Qaderi looks at Iman for a few moments.
After a pause, he writes something on a piece of paper and puts

it on the table so that Iman can read it. Iman looks at the paper. It reads "Listening bugs". Iman looks at Qaderi, Qaderi points to the room with his head. Iman, realizing his own carelessness, looks around.

QADERI

I recommend you read the judges' oath once more.

Iman doesn't know what to say. Qaderi picks up his pack of cigarettes from the table and gets up.

QADERI

Cigarette?

Iman looks at Qaderi.

9. EXT. THE COURTHOUSE YARD- DAY

In a corner of the yard, Iman and Qaderi are standing together and smoking. In the background, now and again soldiers or plainclothes paramilitaries pass, transferring blindfolded prisoners.

QADERI

Do you think you became an investigating judge overnight?

Qaderi takes a drag on his cigarette.

QADERI

The boss doesn't like you. He was against your transfer here right from the beginning. He wanted to bring his person. I insisted. And now he's waiting for the tiniest mistake on your part.

Qaderi puffs on his cigarette. Iman is distressed and confused.

QADERI

Are you trying to undermine me? Or do you want to turn your back on your own progress and success, your wife and children? Do you know how many people were trying to be an investigating judge in this office? How many years you've been waiting to be a judge? Iman, here you have to fight. You have to prove yourself, especially in this case which is a direct order from the prosecutor.

                    IMAN

But I haven't even read the case, how can I issue a punishment for "waging war against God"? and request a death penalty?

                    QADERI

Prosecutor's order... is the law, do you understand?

Iman is deep in his thoughts.

10. INT./EXT. TAILOR'S SHOP AND BAZAAR - DAY

In a tailor's workshop in the bazaar, where a middle-aged lady offers services to several young women and girls.

Wearing a school uniform, Sana opens the door of a fitting room. Sadaf and Rezvan look at her.

                    Rezvan

                It's so nice.

Sadaf pauses and looks more carefully.

                    SADAF

        Look at her shoulders... it doesn't fit her well...

Sana checks the uniform's shoulders in the mirror. Away from Sana's eyes, Sadaf softly whispers something in Rezvan's ear.

                    SADAF

        It's also very baggy in the front.

Rezvan looks at Sana.

                    SADAF

                should I tell her?

                    Rezvan

                    Yeah.

SADAF

Dear ma'am...

TAILOR

Yes, my darling?

SADAF

Thank you very much, it looks very beautiful, but it doesn't fit well on her shoulders and the front is too baggy. The shape of her chest can't be seen at all.

The tailor walks toward Sana. She tries to arrange the shoulders and the front of the dress.

TAILOR

First of all, not chest, they're boobs. The chest is somewhere else. If the front of the dress is tighter than this, they will get in trouble at school. And what difference does it make in how it will fit? It is covered by the headscarf, no one would see it anyway.

SADAF

You are right, but please fix it.

TAILOR

My dear, this is a school uniform, not a party dress!

SADAF

but what would be the problem if her school uniform fit her well too?

The tailor nods and points to Sana.

TAILOR

Take it off, sweety.

SADAF

Now that you're working on it, you're going to fix the front too, right?

                              TAILOR

don't come back later to tell me the school said it's too tight.

                         REZVAN (to Sadaf)

                          let that one go.

                               SANA

What do you mean? No way! I don't like it to be loose like this.

                              REZVAN

              Please fix the front as well. Thank you.

The tailor nods.

                              REZVAN

                      When will it be ready?

                              TAILOR

  Call me next week if it is ready you can come to pick it up.

                               SANA

                 Ma'am, school will start next week.

                              TAILOR

                 What can I do, dear? I'm very busy.

                               SADAF

                        Please make it work.

Rezvan's phone rings. Seeing her mother's name, Rezvan steps
away from the crowd to answer. The conversation between Sadaf,
the tailor, and Sana continues.

                              REZVAN

Hello mom… No, we are at the tailor's, it's not bad, it only
looked a bit puffy on her shoulders, but she'll fix it… No,
we'll be there in an hour, an hour and a half… Ok... do you
remember Sadaf is also with Sana and me… but I told you last
                              week…

Worried that Sadaf will hear this conversation, Rezvan slowly increases her distance.

                        REZVAN

What do you mean Mom? First of all, I told you beforehand. Besides that, Sadaf came from her town and her dorm is not ready yet. She doesn't have anyone here. You agreed in advance and told her she could stay the night at our place.

Sana approaches Rezvan.

                         SANA

                   what happened?

Rezvan shakes her head, emphasizing that it's not important. She moves away from Sana.

                        REZVAN

Mom, I told you. Now, why are you so strict about Sadaf all of a sudden? … Okay.

11. EXT. BAZAAR- DAY

In the market Sana, Rezvan, and Sadaf are walking together among the crowd, going from one shop to another.

12. INT. APT- LIVING ROOM - DAY

Najmeh, Rezvan, Sana, and Sadaf are sitting around the dining table. The meal is over.

                        SADAF

              Thank you so much, Auntie.

                        NAJMEH

         Don't mention it, honey. are you full?

                        SADAF

        Yes, thank you, it was very delicious.

NAJMEH

I'm happy you enjoyed it, dear.

The kids begin to collect the plates and clean the table.

13. INT. APT. KITCHEN. NAJMEH'S BEDROOM- DAY

Kitchen.

Rezvan, Sadaf, and Sana are in the kitchen, doing the dishes. Sadaf is washing, Rezvan rinses and Sana dries and puts them away. While working together, they start talking about what happened at the tailor's shop and the tailor's personality. Najmeh comes out of the room and calls Rezvan. Rezvan stops washing the dishes, dries her hands, and goes to her mother's bedroom.

Najmeh's bedroom. Continuous.

Rezvan enters the bedroom.

REZVAN

Yes, Mom.

NAJMEH

My darling, did your friend eat her food?

Rezvan, surprised, looks at Najmeh.

NAJMEH

I made tea as well. Drink it, stay together for half an hour, then she needs to go, please.

REZVAN

What do you mean Mom? What's going on? do you even hear what I'm saying? her dormitory is not ready, and she doesn't have anyone in Tehran. Do you want to throw her out of the house?

NAJMEH

My dear, tell me what was she going to do if she didn't have a friend named Rezvan?

                         REZVAN

                  Well, she has one now.

                         NAJMEH

  We talked about it. I explained to both of you that the
   circumstances of our family have changed, and we have to be
                         careful.

                         REZVAN

                   Careful about what?

                         NAJMEH

                   About those around us.

                         REZVAN

         In what possible way is Sadaf dangerous for us?

                         NAJMEH

   Why do you think Sadaf is my problem? I'm saying you should
   change your way of life. If you can't tell her, I will go and
                     talk to her myself.

Rezvan looks at Najmeh. The look on her face shows she's
restraining her anger.

                         REZVAN

   Then let me talk to Dad myself and ask for his permission for
                   Sadaf to stay tonight.

                         NAJMEH

   Rezvan, Dad is busy with work, we should not disturb him. Also,
                he entrusted me with such issues.

Rezvan is desperate.

                         REZVAN

   So at least let her stay until the evening... In the meantime, I
                   will tell her somehow.

Najmeh mulls it over.

NAJMEH

Okay, dear. She stays until the evening.

Upset because of her mother's behavior, Rezvan is leaving the room.

REZVAN

Thanks.

Rezvan is about to leave the bedroom.

NAJMEH

Rezvan, why is it so important to you?

Rezvan looks at her mother.

REZVAN

Because she's my friend, she is alone here.

NAJMEH

Even if you solve her problem tonight, what's going to happen the next time her dormitory is not ready?

REZVAN

I don't know, mom. I thought you wouldn't have a problem if she stayed with us for one night, so I told her she could stay here with us. Tomorrow, they will give her a room in the dormitory.

NAJMEH

OK, I'll let her stay tonight on two conditions.

Hora happily runs towards Najmeh.

REZVAN

What conditions?

NAJMEH

The first condition is that you promise it's the last time you make such a request again. The second is that you make sure

Sadaf does not leave the room from the moment Dad comes home until he leaves early in the morning. I don't want her to see your father.

                    REZVAN

               No problem, mom.

Rezvan rushes out of the room.

14. INT. GIRLS' BEDROOM - DAY (EVENING)

In the kids' room, Najmeh is plucking Rezvan's eyebrows. Sadaf is painting Sana's nails. Rezvan is looking at her eyebrows in a small hand mirror.

                    REZVAN

     Mom, this is still too thick, make it thinner.

                    NAJMEH

     If you make it any thinner, you will be like a slut.

                    SADAF

     Auntie... my eyebrows are thin... but swear to God, I'm not a
                   bad girl.

                    NAJMEH

     Oh my God! Of course, not. I didn't mean you. I'm just saying
     that Rezvan is still a daughter of this house. She should be
     more mindful. Whenever she gets married, according to her
           husband's taste, she can do whatever she wants.

                    REZVAN

     So even later I have to do whatever my husband wants? When will
                I do anything for myself?

To show that she is complying with her wishes, Najmeh plucks a few more strands of hair from Rezvan's eyebrow.

                    NAJMEH

               Don't move so much.

SADAF

Although Rezvan, keep in mind that full and natural eyebrows are fashionable now.

REZVAN

Mom, are you plucking my eyebrows for real? I don't feel anything.

As an answer to Rezvan, Najmeh plucks out a hair. Rezvan sighs.

REZVAN

Mom, when should I highlight my hair?

NAJMEH

What do you want to do with such beautiful hair? Don't you hear Sadaf saying that natural is fashionable?

Painting Sana's nails is finished, now Sadaf is busy sticking a fake nose stud on Sana's nose.

REZVAN

Mom! She says natural eyebrows are fashionable.

SANA

I want to dye my hair blue this summer anyway.

NAJMEH

If you turn your hair blue, I sure will turn your life black.

Kids laugh.

NAJMEH

Also, you're going to remove your nail polish tonight before your dad comes. I don't want to deal with such trouble.

SANA

Mom, why are you doing this, don't you dye your hair yourself?

> NAJMEH
>
> Do you understand the difference between a girl and a married woman?

With her painted nails, Sana puts her hands on her face and makes a silly face. Rezvan laughs and because of Rezvan's laughter, Najmeh looks at Sana.

> NAJMEH
>
> What are you doing?

Najmeh's phone rings. Seeing Iman's name, Najmeh gets up in a hurry and leaves the room. Rezvan comes toward Sana. Sadaf takes out a lipstick from her bag and starts rubbing it on Sana's lips.

> SADAF
>
> Let me make you pretty...Rezvan...Does your mom hate me?

> REZVAN
>
> Why would you say that?

> SADAF
>
> Don't you see that she is constantly throwing shades at me?

> REZVAN
>
> No, come on! She doesn't mean you. She is worried about Sana's behavior.

Sana with curly hair, a stud on her nose, and a bright lipstick on her lips, while holding her hands so that her nail polish is visible, pretend to be dancing Bandari. Rezvan and Sadaf are laughing.

15. INT.LIVING ROOM- MIDNIGHT

Najmeh has fallen asleep on the sofa. The TV is on. After a few moments, the sound of the key turning in the lock is heard, followed by the opening of the door. Najmeh wakes up. Iman enters confused and tired. Seeing him, Najmeh goes towards him.

                              NAJMEH

                          It's very late.

Exhausted, Iman hands his bag to Najmeh and without saying a
word, goes to the bathroom.

                              NAJMEH

                          Are you okay?

Iman nods and enters the bathroom. Najmeh runs to the room. She
puts the bag down and pauses for a moment. Then she turns toward
the bathroom. She tries to enter but the bathroom door is
locked. She knocks on the door several times but doesn't get any
response.

16. INT. APT. BATHROOM - MIDNIGHT

In the shower, Iman is holding his face under the water. Drops
of water are hitting his face.

Iman is standing in a corner and staring at the ground with his
hand stretched out as support. Water is dripping from his face.
He picks up and wears his towel. It seems that he is trying to
calm down. He leaves the bathroom. A bit farther in the
background, we can see a gun that Iman left next to the sink.

17. INT. BEDROOM- NIGHT

In the darkness of the room, Iman is standing near the window
and staring out. Najmeh arrives with a tray of hot food. She
puts food on a plate for Iman and tries to feed him. Iman
doesn't eat any. Eventually, Najmeh stops trying.

                              NAJMEH

                       What's going on, honey?

In silence, Iman is looking out the window.

                              NAJMEH

                       Why don't you tell me?

Iman looks at Najmeh.

> IMAN
>
> Why do you think they chose me as an investigating judge?

Looking at Iman, Najmeh waits for him to continue.

> IMAN
>
> They think I will do whatever they ask me.

> NAJMEH
>
> Who?

> IMAN
>
> The previous investigating judge was fired when he did not sign the execution sentence of a defendant... Why didn't he sign it? Maybe the accused is innocent.

Najmeh doesn't know what to say. She is fretful.

> NAJMEH
>
> Did they ask you to do something?

Iman stares into Najmeh's eyes for a while.

> IMAN
>
> They want me to sign off on that death penalty sentence.

> NAJMEH
>
> Unjust execution?

> IMAN
>
> I don't know.

> NAJMEH
>
> Do not sign that.

Iman looks at Najmeh.

                              IMAN

              The prosecutor's order is... the law.

                             NAJMEH

    So, if the prosecutor gave the order, it has nothing to do with
                            you, right?

                              IMAN

       Qaderi says this is the original verdict... if there is any
       defect in the case, then there is a retrial, and after that the
       court of appeal... and then the resumption of proceedings...

A noise comes from the children's room. Najmeh becomes restless.

                             NAJMEH

                 Let it go for now. Let's go and rest.

18. INT. APT. KITCHEN TO BEDROOM - NIGHT

On a plate, Najmeh puts a glass of water next to a pill and goes toward the bedroom. On her way, she notices that one of the girls has been in the bathroom and is now going back to their room, closing the door. Najmeh can't tell who it was. She enters the bedroom, gives Iman a pill, and puts him to sleep. After pulling the blanket over him, Najmeh goes to the bathroom.

In the bathroom, she starts collecting Iman's clothes. Suddenly, she notices the gun that Iman left there on the dresser. Terrified, Najmeh looks out the door, making sure no one is there. She picks up the gun and puts it in the dirty laundry. Sneaking out of the bathroom, she goes back to the bedroom. Iman is in deep sleep. Najmeh puts the gun in the drawer next to him. She comes out of the room again with the dirty laundry and goes toward the washing machine. As she is putting the clothes in the washing machine one by one, she suddenly notices a blood-like stain on Iman's shirt. She thinks about it for a while, but soon she decides to look the other way and throws the rest of the laundry in the washing machine.

19. INT. APT. NAJMEH'S BEDROOM – DAY

hearing the phone ringing, Najmeh wakes up. Iman is on the line.

NAJMEH

Hello () Hello, do you feel better? () Oh, good, thank God () No, I couldn't sleep last night () I fell asleep near dawn () where? () why?

Najmeh gets up and sits on the bed.

NAJMEH

No, in the afternoon, the kids and I are going to do some shopping together. Rezvan needs to buy some clothes for the university, and Sana also wants to buy her school stationery () okay () no, if it's like what you're saying, we won't go () okay.

20. INT. APT. LIVING ROOM– DAY

Najmeh, Rezvan, and Sana are in the living room. Rezvan and Sana are sitting on each corner of the sofa, with their phones in their hands. Something's off about the situation. While drinking tea, Najmeh is watching the TV report of the protests. A one-sided report from Iran's state television describes the protesters as violent agitators and rioters. Rezvan too is watching the reports carefully. But Sana is on her phone watching the protest footage recorded by people, without paying attention to the TV. Now and then she takes a glance at the TV, and at Rezvan and Najmeh, who are attentively following the report. Sana copies the link to the video she's watching and sends it to Rezvan. Rezvan notices she received a text. Seeing Sana's name, she is surprised that she is only a few steps away but still has sent a text message. Only by using eye gestures, Rezvan asks her what the link is. Away from Najmeh's eyes, Sana responds with a look that she must check out the link.
Rezvan opens the link and watches the video. Sana writes a message to Rezvan, saying "Do you see how they are beating up people? But look what they're showing on TV! They're constantly lying". Rezvan responds with a sad emoji. Sana writes "Sadaf didn't reach the dormitory?" Rezvan writes "No, she hasn't texted me yet". Sana sends her another video. Rezvan watches. The plainclothesmen forces are beating up a girl who's

protesting without hijab. One of the men grabs the girl's hair and drags her to the ground and throws her into a police van. **The image on Rezvan's mobile screen cuts to documentary videos of police violence against women. (recorded with mobile phones)**

21. INT./EXT. APT. BEDROOM. LIVINGROOM - NIGHT

Living room.

With its tall windows, the apartment looks like a prison from the outside. While holding her phone (on speaker), Najmeh is waiting behind the living room window for Iman to answer his phone. *Death to the dictator* chant can be heard from outside. Although the number of chanters is not many, these voices get Najmeh thinking. Her call remains unanswered, and she closes the window. Restless and nervous, she walks toward the stove and turns off the burner.

Girls' room.

Rezvan and Sana are listening to the slogans through the window. Rezvan's phone rings.

>REZVAN
>
>Sadaf!

Rezvan answers. Sana asks her to put it on speaker. Rezvan does so.

>REZVAN
>
>Are they chanting there too?

>SADAF
>
>Yes, many are!

Through the phone, you can hear people shouting *death to the dictator* close by. Sadaf is speaking with excitement and joy. Occasionally, she bursts into laughter with happiness as she speaks.

>REZVAN
>
>in the dormitory too?

SADAF

can't you hear it? Listen!

Sadaf stays silent for a moment. Students' chants can be heard through the phone.

SANA

Did you chant as well?

SADAF

I chanted and took off my scarf too.

REZVAN

no way!

SANA

Bravo!

Sana and Rezvan are excited. Sadaf shouts *death to the dictator*. Her voice is very loud on the phone. Rezvan, afraid of her voice being heard, cancels the speaker mode, and holds the phone to her ears.

REZVAN

What are you doing Sadaf? My mom will show up now.

Sadaf laughs.

SADAF

See how many files I've sent. Go and watch them.

REZVAN

Everything has been filtered since this evening though.

SADAF

I will send you a VPN now.

SANA

                    Send it to me too.

Rezvan hangs up the phone.

                         REZVAN

    What are you saying? Do you have to do everything that I do?

                          SANA

              Well, I want to use the Internet too.

Rezvan leaves the bedroom.

22. INT. APT. LIVING ROOM - NIGHT

Rezvan and Sana are having dinner with Najmeh.

                         REZVAN

            It is not possible to stay home all the time.

                         NAJMEH

    You've been staying home for just one day now, what's all this
            fuss about? Don't you see what's going on?

                          SANA

          what's going on Mom? People are living their lives.

                         NAJMEH

    Why do you two think you understand everything better than me
    and your father? is this life? Breaking the glass, setting
                        things on fire.

                         REZVAN

    It's not all about breaking glass and setting things on fire.
    People are protesting. They don't let them protest, they break
         the glass, throw tear gas at them, and start a fire.

Najmeh gives Rezvan a fierce glare.

                         NAJMEH

    Well, great! Now you've become the defender of the rioters.

As the news program starts on TV, Najmeh picks up the remote and turns up the volume.

NAJMEH

Be quiet, I wanna see what the news says.

Away from the dinner table, Najmeh is watching the news on TV… It is not only Najmeh who is caught up in the images and the reports. Rezvan is also watching carefully.

REZVAN

Did they really kill someone because of hijab?

Najmeh looks at her.

NAJMEH

She had a stroke. It says that she's been sick already.

REZVAN

Who knows?

NAJMEH

He is saying it on TV.

SANA

Whatever they say on TV is true?

NAJMEH

No, whatever you say is true! Listen, it's saying that she had a heart problem. She had a stroke while in the custody of the morality police.

REZVAN

Well, she must have been so scared that she ended up having a stroke.

NAJMEH

Thousands of people have heart attacks every day, is it the government's fault?

REZVAN

Thousands of people are not having heart attacks out of fear from the police.

SANA

Would you say the same thing if she was your own daughter?

NAJMEH

My daughter wouldn't dare to go out dressed like that.

REZVAN

Why should someone be arrested for their clothes in the first place?

NAJMEH

Because it is God's order. It is the law of the land.

SANA

Well, maybe the law is wrong.

NAJMEH

God's law is infallible.

REZVAN

Who assured you that this is God's law anyway?

NAJMEH

What's going on with you two? Well go on then, get up and go start chanting in the street. Go and dance bareheaded in the middle of the street. Your father has no idea what is going on in this house.

Najmeh leaves the dinner table. Rezvan and Sana are astonished by Najmeh's irrational behavior.

SANA

What is she saying? Why does she act like that?

REZVAN

I don't know. Why do we argue with her when we know she doesn't accept anything?

23. INT. BEDROOM- MIDNIGHT

Iman and Najmeh are in bed. They talk softly in the dark of the room.

NAJMEH

The kids have grown up. They have ideas and questions. They need you. You know what? I don't want anything from you. But a girl at this age needs her father, they get bored...

IMAN

It's gonna be like this just for a short while, it will be ok. Schools and universities are about to begin as well, kids will be busy studying. Be patient a bit longer.

Najmeh pauses for a moment.

NAJMEH

Iman…

IMAN

Yes, my darling?

NAJMEH

Did you sign off on that death penalty sentence?

IMAN

Yeah...

Taken by surprise, Najmeh turns toward Iman.

IMAN

I thought about it a lot. I was being emotional. I mixed my ego's desires with the execution of God's decree.

With these explanations, Najmeh is reassured.

                              IMAN

        A self-sacrifice is necessary, to be able to
        submit oneself to God's law. "I am at peace with
          those who are at peace with you and at war with
             those who fight you, until the Day of
                            Resurrection."

In silence, Najmeh is eagerly listening to Iman's words.

                             NAJMEH

                       Did you fall asleep?

Iman answers drowsily.

                              IMAN

                          I'm about to.

                             NAJMEH

        I know now is not a good time, but we may not be able to talk
                             again soon.

                              IMAN

                            Tell me.

                             NAJMEH

Remember you promised to buy a dishwasher in a good opportunity?
The hands of me and the girls are getting damaged. Can't we do
                            it sooner?

                              IMAN

        sure honey, next week we'll go and buy it together.

Najmeh embraces Iman.

24. INT. APT. LIVING ROOM- DAWN

In the living room, before sunrise, while the city can be seen
through the tall windows of the living room, Iman is praying,

and behind him stands Najmeh, following his lead. She repeats everything Iman does with a short delay.

25. INT./EXT. NAJMEH'S CAR. TEHRAN'S STREETS- DAY

Najmeh, Sana, and Rezvan are driving to school. Sana is wearing the uniform and scarf that we've seen before. Rezvan is also wearing clothes suitable for the university, with a full hijab. Radio broadcasts a live show about the first day of school.

NAJMEH

Did you take your fruit and sandwich?

SANA

Yes, Mom. I did.

NAJMEH

Water bottle? I left it in the fridge for you last night.

SANA

No, I forgot that.

NAJMEH

Do I have to remind you about that too? Buy mineral water, don't drink water from the tap.

SANA

OK, Mom, I'm not a child.

Najmeh stops the car in front of Sana's school. Sana gets out of the car.

NAJMEH

Keep your phone in your backpack, don't get in trouble for it.

SANA

No, Mom, I won't.

NAJMEH

I will pick you up at one o'clock.

SANA

OK, bye.

Rezvan and Najmeh say goodbye to Sana. Najmeh drives away. After a few moments, Najmeh turns down the volume of the radio.

NAJMEH

Rezvan, weren't you supposed to keep a proper distance from your friends?

REZVAN

Ma, Sadaf is my only friend.

NAJMEH

Am I saying she can't be your friend? I say be careful because of your father's job conditions.

REZVAN

Mom, I don't understand. What do you exactly mean by Dad's job conditions? What conditions does it have?

NAJMEH

Dad's work is sensitive. Just like your uncle. Your uncle is always traveling, right? But does anyone know where he is? Do you know exactly what your uncle's job is? I don't know, and I'm his sister. I only know that he is in the military.

REZVAN

After all, is Dad a judge, an investigating judge, or a military man?

NAJMEH

I'm saying his job is just as sensitive. We should not draw too much attention to ourselves. When you get close to people, you might say something by accident that you shouldn't. Why did you plan last night to pick up Sadaf today?

                              REZVAN

     Mom, Sadaf's dormitory is on our way! Also, you said she
        shouldn't come to our home. I'm 21 years old and you're
                    controlling all my relationships.

                              NAJMEH

         Controlling? I'm protecting the family. Inshallah, when you
               become a mother, you'll know what I mean.

                              REZVAN

                    There she is. Sadaf is standing there.

Najmeh stops. Sadaf gets in the car.

                              SADAF

                       Hello Auntie, hello Rezvan.

                              REZVAN

                                Hello.

                              NAJMEH

          Hello dear, how are you? How are your parents?

                              SADAF

     Fine, thank you. Actually, I was just speaking to my mom on the
         phone, they sent their regards. Sorry for the trouble.

                              NAJMEH

       It's so kind of them. No honey, not a problem, it was on our
                                 way.

                              SADAF

     Wow, you have no idea what was going on in the dormitory last
                                night.

                              NAJMEH

                            what happened?

Sitting in the front seat, Rezvan puts her hand behind the seat and tries to stop Sadaf from sharing more. Sadaf notices Rezvan's warning.

SADAF

It was crowded, everyone was chanting.

NAJMEH

Did you chant too?

REZVAN

Sadaf, you were talking to your mom, are there protests there as well?

SADAF

Yes, it seems like people everywhere are quite angry.

26. EXT. STREET- DAY (CONTINUOUS)

Najmeh stops at a corner of the street, and Rezvan and Sadaf get out of the car. Sadaf thanks Najmeh and says goodbye. Rezvan says goodbye to her mother and together they walk across the street. Najmeh watches them go. It seems that something has worried her.

27. INT./EXT. STREET - DAY

Najmeh is driving back towards home. Her phone rings. We hear the conversation on the car's speaker.

SANA

Mom…

NAJMEH

What's going on dear?

SANA

Come and pick me up, they say the school is closed.

NAJMEH

Why dear? what happened?

SANA

It's because of the protests. The girls are chanting.

NAJMEH

Okay. I'll turn around right away, do not join them.

SANA

Come.

Najmeh starts dialing Rezvan's number. Rezvan's phone is not available. Najmeh arrives in front of the school. Sana, seeing her mother's car, runs towards her and gets in.

NAJMEH

What was going on, sweety?

SANA

I don't know. Kids were chanting.

NAJMEH

What was the slogan?

SANA

Women, life, freedom.

NAJMEH

Call Rezvan. I tried several times, but her phone was not available.

Sana starts dialing Rezvan's number. The radio host is still talking about the first day of school and the beginning of the school year.

SANA

Not available.

NAJMEH

Why?

SANA

Maybe the battery is dead.

NAJMEH

Early in the morning? We'll go after her, maybe by the time we get there she'll have service again.

Najmeh is driving hurriedly. She hits the traffic. Entering an alley to skip the traffic, a motorcycle comes towards her car from the opposite direction. shouting.

MOTORCYCLIST

Go back, don't go this way.

NAJMEH

what did he say?

SANA

He said don't go this way.

Several other motorcyclists suddenly pass by Najmeh's car. Najmeh turns back to the street. Upon entering the street, they notice a conflict between people and the police forces. The crowded street does not allow them to move fast. Najmeh and Sana look around in shock.

"The image cuts to documentary videos (recorded with mobile phones). The footages shows widespread student protests at the university and surrounding streets. The police launch an attack."

28. INT. APT. ELEVATOR. LOBBY- DAY

Najmeh and Sana enter the apartment. Najmeh is frantic with fear. Sana rushes to the bedroom, she makes sure her mother is not following her. Najmeh runs toward the TV and turns it on.

SANA

Rezvan? Rezvan...

Sana returns to the living room. A comedy show is on. Najmeh changes the channels, but there is no news about people's protests or any related events. Najmeh's phone rings.

NAJMEH

Iman, what happened? () From what time? () you mean there was no one at the university to say what time they closed the university? () If that's the case, she should have reached home by now. () okay. Okay. () whatever comes up I'll let you know.

Najmeh hangs up the phone and is pensive. Sana notices a message has popped up on her phone. She sneaks into the bathroom to talk to Rezvan away from her mother. She calls Rezvan and starts speaking quietly.

SANA

what happened? Where are you now? () We've been here for a few minutes. () Okay, I'll see what I can do.

Sana contemplates for a second. She then comes out of the bathroom and goes toward the sofa with her hand on her belly. Seeing Sana's state, Najmeh goes toward her.

NAJMEH

are you okay?

SANA

I got my period and I'm out of pads.

NAJMEH

I have a bunch; I bring them right now.

SANA

Mom, sorry, but I need the small size. I can't use your pads. If you can't go to buy it, I will go myself.

NAJMEH

Go and buy it yourself? You have no modesty, do you?

Najmeh leaves the apartment wearing a chador. Sana runs to the window. Looking at the entrance of the parking lot, she dials Rezvan's number. Rezvan picks up the phone.

                    SANA

        she is coming out of the parking lot now...

Najmeh's car drives out of the car park and leaves the building.

                    SANA

                I'm coming down.

Sana hangs up the phone and leaves the apartment.

Elevator. Continuous.

Sana gets out of the elevator on the ground floor and reaches the entrance. She opens the entrance door to the building. Rezvan and Sadaf enter. Half of Sadaf's face is covered with a scarf.

Hallway to the bedroom. Continuous.

Sana and Rezvan are helping Sadaf to get to the elevator. Sadaf's lips are dry, but she tries to pretend it's not a big deal.

bedroom.

Rezvan helps Sadaf lie on the bed. Sana brings her some water and helps her with drinking. She then leaves the room and points to Rezvan to follow her as well.

Living room.

Both Rezvan and Sana come to the living room so they can talk.

                    SANA

        It is dangerous, we must take her to a hospital.

                    REZVAN

        She says no hospital, they will arrest her.

                    SANA

        She says that, so what? What if something happens to her?

REZVAN

Do you think if they arrest her, they will let her stay in the hospital? No one knows what will happen to her.

SANA

Maybe we can find a safe doctor to visit her here.

REZVAN

Who can be trusted?

Najmeh turns the key in the door lock. Rezvan and Sana look at the door.

REZVAN

The only way is to tell Mom to help us.

SANA

Mom? what do you want to say?

REZVAN

We have to tell the truth, there is no other way.

Najmeh opens the door and enters the apartment. She is surprised to see Rezvan.

NAJMEH

Oh, why didn't you call me? I was worried to death.

REZVAN

I just arrived; we got stuck in the crowd. They cut off the mobile phone network.

NAJMEH

Thank God you're okay. Here are your pads. I'm going to call your father, he is worried.

Najmeh passes a black plastic bag to Sana, with the sanitary pads in it. She dials Iman's number on her phone. Going toward the bedroom, Rezvan and Sana stop in the hallway that leads to it.

> NAJMEH

My dear, Rezvan has arrived...it's been crowded, the cut of the mobile phone network around the university...don't worry. Goodbye.

Rezvan and Sana are wondering how to handle the situation. Rezvan comes from the hallway towards Najmeh.

> REZVAN

> Mom...

Najmeh looks at Rezvan.

> NAJMEH

> What's going on?

Rezvan pauses.

> Rezvan

> Sadaf is here.

Najmeh tries to control her anger.

> NAJMEH

> It's like you don't want to take my words seriously.

> REZVAN

> Mom, Sadaf is injured.

Najmeh is shocked.

> NAJMEH

> Where?

Bedroom.

Rezvan, Sana, and Najmeh rush into the bedroom. Sadaf is lying on the bed, and it's obvious that she is in pain. She is breathing with difficulty. Najmeh removes her scarf that covers part of her face. Her face is covered with blood. Seeing the metal pellet scars, Najmeh shudders.

Kitchen.

Najmeh quickly takes cotton balls, gauze, and disinfectant liquid from a cabinet and pours hot water into a small pan.

Bedroom.

Najmeh carefully and patiently washes Sadaf's wounds much like a nurse. Sana and Rezvan look at each other, amazed by their mother's reaction. It's as if they know Najmeh's general attitude and are content that she didn't react badly.

Living room.

Najmeh, Rezvan, and Sana are sitting together in silence.

NAJMEH

It is a huge responsibility... if something happens to her, who will answer her family?

REZVAN

Well, she doesn't want her family to know. It's none of our business.

NAJMEH

Why?

REZVAN

I don't know, but I can see her condition is urgent, something must be done.

NAJMEH

I can't allow that, it's a big responsibility...

REZVAN

To be responsible is not to be indifferent to a wounded person.

NAJMEH

What does it have to do with me? Or you? It's her fault. She could choose not to go, not do anything of that sort.

                              REZVAN

Not to go where? We didn't do anything; we were coming back from the university.

                              NAJMEH

Enough is enough...this house is not a place to do such things! Think about your father. You're responsible toward him as well, not only toward your friends.

Najmeh, Rezvan, and Sana suddenly notice Sadaf's presence. She is standing there, leaning her hand on a wall while looking at them. Sana and Rezvan rush toward her. They want to help, but Sadaf prefers to walk by herself. She goes toward the door. Rezvan and Sana accompany her.

                              REZVAN

Why did you come out? You need to rest.

                              NAJMEH

Sadaf, you should call your mom and let her know what happened.

While breathing heavily, Sadaf walks toward the entrance door. She responds slowly and with difficulty.

                              SADAF

I'm fine, I'll go to the dormitory and rest. Then I'll call my mom.

                              REZVAN

Go back to the bedroom, Sadaf.

Without paying attention to Rezvan's words, Sadaf keeps walking.

                              SANA

Sadaf, you're not fine. You should see a doctor as soon as possible.

                          NAJMEH

            Dear, do you want me to drive you there?

                          SADAF

                   No, I will go myself.

Rezvan looks at her mother in rage. Najmeh calmly goes toward
the door.

                          NAJMEH

         I'm going to get her a taxi, don't come out.

Rezvan goes to the room. Sana is quietly observing everything.
Despite Sadaf's reluctance, Najmeh supports her shoulders so she
can walk and get out of the apartment. They get out and Najmeh
closes the door. Sana is staring at the closed door.

29. INT. APT. GIRLS' BEDROOM - DAY

With headphones on, Sana is listening to *Sara Lov*'s song, *Rain Up*, and looking at Rezvan on a stationary bike in the corner of the room. Rezvan is pressing the pedals with all her strength. Sana is watching her. Suddenly, Rezvan stops, falls on the bike's handlebars, and breaks down in tears. Sana looks at her for a while, then pulls the blanket over her head. As if she knows there is no other choice but to cry.

30. INT. APT- NIGHT

Living room.

It's the middle of the night. Najmeh has fallen asleep in front of the TV. Iman enters the apartment. He gets close to Najmeh. She's in deep sleep. Iman looks at the TV that is on but muted. He walks towards the bedroom, trying not to make any noise.

Bedroom.

Iman takes off his jacket in the dim light that shines into the room from outside. He puts his gun in the drawer and starts unbuttoning his shirt.

Bathroom.

Iman washes his hands and face and looks at himself in the mirror. It seems that something is bothering him. He opens the bathroom door to return to the living room. Najmeh is standing in front of the door. Iman is surprised to see her there.

            NAJMEH

    Your work has changed, have you changed too?

Iman looks at Najmeh. But he has nothing to say.

            NAJMEH

    Why didn't you answer your phone?

            IMAN

    I was in a meeting.

Iman goes to the living room. Najmeh follows him.

In front of the bathroom to the living room.

            NAJMEH

    What about after the meeting? Didn't you see I called?

Iman sits on the sofa.

            IMAN

    Today... Today I had a complicated case. My mind was pretty occupied.

            NAJMEH

    How complicated was it? As much as to forget about your wife and children?

Iman looks at Najmeh.

            IMAN

    A 20-year-old boy... You know, no matter how strong you are, no matter how strong your faith is, execution cases will still get to you...

Najmeh is staring at Iman.

IMAN

On the other hand, unfortunately, this chaos coincided with the beginning of my work in this branch. The number of detainees is very high. Fourteen- and fifteen-year-old kids to seventy-year-old men and women. And it's increasing every day. There's no more room in prisons. They're asking us to clarify the status of the detainees as soon as possible. In a minute or two, I should be able to explain the charges and make a decision. One hundred, two hundred, or three hundred a day... I don't know.

NAJMEH

There is always work. Do you know when was the last time we sat at the same table with the kids?

IMAN

You explain to them and calm them down.

NAJMEH

Who will calm me down?

Iman is silent. He looks at Najmeh.

NAJMEH

Can you please spend some time with the kids tomorrow morning before you leave?

Iman nods.

IMAN

I like to very much, but I must be at the prosecutor's office early in the morning. Tomorrow night… Tomorrow night I will come home early so that we can have dinner together.

Najmeh's reaction shows she is not pleased with this answer but seems to accept it anyway.

IMAN

By the way, don't let them go to school or university until I tell you otherwise.

                              NAJMEH

            How can they not go to school and university?

                               IMAN

       The government closed them for the time being, but they are not
                           going to announce it.

Rezvan suddenly rushes out of the bedroom.

                              REZVAN

                            Mom... mom...

Seeing her father, Rezvan greets him briefly and mindlessly.

                              REZVAN

                       Hi dad, how are you?

                 Mom, would you come here for a second?

                               IMAN

                         Did something happen?

                              NAJMEH

                Yes, dear. Go, I'm right behind you.

Najmeh tries to reassure Iman.

                              NAJMEH

 It's okay, they must have had an argument, I'll be back quickly.

Najmeh follows Rezvan to their bedroom.

Room.

Najmeh enters the room. Stunned, Sana is sitting on her bed and
looks at Najmeh and Rezvan. Rezvan shows a video to Najmeh on
her phone. In the video, which seems to have been recorded
secretly, the plainclothesmen are forcefully taking Sadaf away
from the dorm.

                              NAJMEH

                           what is this?

REZVAN

You see? I told you not to let her go. Girls from the dormitory recorded this video. They took Sadaf.

Najmeh stays silent for a while. She returns the phone to Rezvan.

NAJMEH

Don't you see that I was right? If she stayed here, now they were raiding our house! Then what could you tell your father?

Rezvan is leaving the room.

REZVAN

I'll talk to Dad myself.

Najmeh stops her.

NAJMEH
Where are you going?
Wait, what are you doing?

REZVAN

I want to talk to Dad.

NAJMEH

what do you want to say?

REZVAN

I want to know where they took her. No one knows who they were, or where they took her. What has Sadaf done?

NAJMEH

Quiet. Do you think your father knows about these things?

SANA

who knows then?

Najmeh just noticed Sana's presence. She looks at her.

NAJMEH

You're just a kid. Why do you interfere in these matters? Well, both of you, listen carefully. This girl must have done something, the agents do not arrest someone for no reason, especially like this.

                    REZVAN

She didn't do anything; I was with her.

                    NAJMEH

This is the last time you say you were with her. You weren't with her anywhere!

Iman's voice can be heard from outside.

                    IMAN

Najmeh...

Najmeh notices he's calling, and she responds loudly.

                    NAJMEH

I'm coming.

She turns toward the kids and starts speaking quietly, in a stern and scolding tone.

                    NAJMEH

I will follow up tomorrow morning first thing through an acquaintance. Wherever she is, I will find her by noon. Don't worry. Cell phones are off, now! go back to sleep.

Najmeh turns off the light and leaves the room. She closes the door behind her. The room plunges into darkness.

31. INT. GIRLS' BEDROOM- NIGHT

Sana is in Rezvan's bed. They are watching videos of the protests together. Some of the videos excite them. Some make them sad. The light of the phone screens shines on their faces.

"The image cuts to documentary videos (recorded with mobile phones). The footages shows the widespread crackdown on

protesters by the police, with excessive violence and the death of demonstrators."

32. INT./EXT. NAJMEH'S CAR. STREET – DAY

Najmeh is driving in the street. While passing by, she sees clashes breaking between people and the repression forces. Najmeh turns into an alley and stops a little later. She takes out her phone and sends a text message. Several vans enter from the other side of the alley and then enter a house's parking space. Najmeh looks at the vans. It's not possible to see inside of the vans. From the same ordinary house, comes out a woman wearing a chador and a mask on her face. She looks around and sees Najmeh's car. The woman comes toward the car and then gets in. Najmeh and her friend, Faati, kiss and say hello.

NAJMEH

how are you honey, how is Alireza?

FAATI

We are not doing bad, thank God. You've seen the situation yourself.

Faati points to the vans.

FAATI

Alireza said Iman has become an investigating judge at the prosecutor's office. Congratulations.

NAJMEH

Yes, thank you, dear. What can I say, until now it has been nothing but trouble. He is so caught up...

FAATI

Don't be ungrateful, do you know how much his salary will increase? He will only stay at the prosecutor's office for a year or two. God willing, he will soon be transferred to the Revolutionary Court and become the head judge of the branch. Wow, do you know what it's like to be a judge's wife? If he becomes a judge, your situation will be even better than it is.

NAJMEH

I hope it happens for you and Alireza too.

FAATI

We are busy here from morning to night. You don't know what's going on. They keep bringing people in.

NAJMEH

yes, I heard. To be honest, I'm here about something related. the daughter of an acquaintance was arrested too and there's no sign of her.

FAATI

when they arrested her?

NAJMEH

Last night. They raided the university dormitory. They took her as well. her family is from another town.

FAATI

Who were they? Plainclothesmen or anti-riot?

NAJMEH

Apparently, plainclothesmen.

FAATI

If they were plainclothesmen, God help us. She can't be found this soon.

NAJMEH

To be honest, she was shot and injured a few hours before the arrest, that's why her family is very worried about her and I'm disturbing you. I thought maybe you could take a look in your system and tell us where she is...

Faati pauses a little.

FAATI

I can't promise anything, but give me her name, details, and National ID Number and I'll see what I can do.

Two more vans arrive to enter the safe house. Seeing the vans, Faati decides to leave. She remembers something before getting off.

FAATI

My dear, I have to go, you see what's going on.

NAJMEH

Thank you so much, thank you for your time.

FAATI

Dear Najmeh, I don't want to pry, but be more careful. These friends and acquaintances who make such demands of you... their children will go to riots, something happens to them, then they suddenly think...

Najmeh is surprised by Faati's words.

FAATI

Truth be told, some godless people have been identifying names, addresses, phone numbers, and details of investigating judges and judges, and in short, anyone who is serving this system. And they are posting them on Instagram, Facebook, and cyberspace, whatever. From there, it gets to enemy networks. Please don't get upset but be careful. Do not hang out with everyone.

Confused, Najmeh is looking at Faati.

NAJMEH

No, you are right, we're careful.

FAATI

great dear, say hello.

NAJMEH

Excuse me, Faati, can you please not tell Alireza that I asked you this? I'm afraid he tells Iman and then Iman gets upset about it. Don't even say we met. I don't want anyone to know.

                          FAATI

              OK, honey, I won't say a word.

Faati closes the door and leaves. Najmeh watches her leave.

33. INT. APT- DAY

Najmeh enters the apartment. Sana and Rezvan run towards her.

                         REZVAN

                     what happened?

                         NAJMEH

            They need her National ID Number.

                         REZVAN

             How can we find her ID Number?

                         NAJMEH

I don't know, you talk as if it's my fault they arrested her.
She went out in the streets, broke banks' windows, set tires on
  fire, and did whatever she wanted. It's her fault, she chose
                 this herself. Call her family.

                         REZVAN

Mom, don't you understand what I'm saying, I was with her, she
                     didn't do anything.

                          SANA

Mom, Rezvan was standing beside her. Those pellets could've hit
                        Rezvan's eyes.

                         NAJMEH

Rezvan doesn't dare to get in trouble, joining a riot. These are
    a bunch of thugs coming to the streets to run naked.

Rezvan's phone rings. Rezvan answers.

REZVAN

Hello, is there any news? () unfortunately, no, my search was also unsuccessful.

Najmeh starts listening carefully to the conversation.

REZVAN

Now we need her National ID Number to continue the search () ask others, maybe someone has it () OK then, I'm waiting, send it to me.

Rezvan hangs up the phone. Burning with anger, Najmeh turns Rezvan.

NAJMEH

what the hell are you doing? Who were you talking to?

REZVAN

Mom, what are you talking about? I was speaking to my classmate.

NAJMEH

Did you tell someone you can do something? Did you talk about your father?

REZVAN

What do you mean?

NAJMEH

You're playing dumb? What did you tell your friends? Did you say how are you looking for her?

REZVAN

I did not mention Dad's name or his job.

NAJMEH

what did you say then?

                            REZVAN

            I said my uncle has an acquaintance.

Rezvan goes toward her room. Najmeh follows her.

                            NAJMEH

You had no right to mention your uncle's name. I swear to God,
   if I find out you said one word about your father… or your
                             uncle…

                            REZVAN

  I did not say anything to anyone. I know what to say and what
      not to say. I swear I leave this house and go away.

                            NAJMEH

Wow! Since when do you say such things? Where do you think you
     are? Do you think you can do whatever you want?

Rezvan closes the door of the room. Najmeh knocks on the door.

                            NAJMEH

                  Do not close the door.

                             SANA

               Mom, for god's sake, let it go.

                            NAJMEH

What? Let it go? do you think you can do whatever in this house?
  I will tell your father everything tonight, then it's between
                         you and him.

Najmeh goes to her room. Confused, Sana leans against the wall.

34. INT. APT. KITCHEN- DAY (NEARLY NIGHT)

Najmeh and Sana are in the kitchen, cooking. Najmeh's
interactions with Sana are accompanied by boredom. She keeps
telling Sana what to do. Sana patiently listens to her words and
helps with the cooking. The TV is on. Najmeh and Sana are

draining the rice, and frying eggplants, potatoes, and chicken. They are stirring Gheimeh stew.

35. INT. APT. LIVING ROOM- NIGHT

Najmeh is alone in the living room. The lights are half lit. Najmeh is carefully watching the 9 o'clock news show on TV. She then turns off the TV and picks up her phone to call Iman, but she changes her mind. She goes to the kitchen. She turns off the stove burners and leaves the kitchen.

36. INT. NAJMEH'S BEDROOM- NIGHT

In the dark, Najmeh is standing by the window and listening to the sound of people chanting. It seems the number of people chanting is more than before, and the sound is very close now. She sticks her head out of the window to see which neighbor has joined the chanters. She listens for a while. Suddenly, Iman enters the room.

                    IMAN

        what has happened?

Najmeh looks back.

                    NAJMEH

        you came. I thought you forgot...

Iman nods. He seems very tired. He goes toward the drawer and puts his bag in a corner.

                    NAJMEH

        do you hear that? One of the neighbors is chanting...

Iman looks at Najmeh. He takes off his jacket and throws it on the bed. He takes out the gun from behind his back and puts it in the drawer. He then goes toward Najmeh.

                    IMAN

>   These dirtbags... eat this regime's salt and then chant slogans
>   against it too. We'll get rid of them.

Now both of them are standing together near the window and listening to the slogan of *death to the dictator*.

>   NAJMEH
>
>   There are many, Iman. do you hear them?

They both listen for a while.

>   NAJMEH
>
>   What if something happens?

>   IMAN
>
>   Like what?

>   NAJMEH
>
>   I mean, you've never thought about it?

Iman is silent. It seems that the answer is he did but doesn't want to say it out loud.

>   NAJMEH
>
>   I'm afraid. What will they do to us if something happens?

Iman closes the window.

>   IMAN
>
>   Nothing's going to happen...

>   NAJMEH
>
>   How can you be sure?

>   IMAN
>
> We won't allow it... whoever stands in the way of God's religion
>   is responsible for his life.

Hearing Iman's words, Najmeh pauses a little.

>   NAJMEH

>   There are protests everywhere, even
>   in universities and schools.

Iman takes a breath and shakes his head.

> IMAN
>
> I know... where are the kids?

> NAJMEH
>
> In their room... they are upset. They arrested some of Rezvan's classmates.

Iman gets worried.

> IMAN
>
> Rezvan wasn't in these riots, was she?

> NAJMEH
>
> No, she wasn't. But they took one of her close friends. she is worried about her and is very sad. She doesn't come out of the room.

Iman takes a glance at Najmeh.

> NAJMEH
> Does anyone know who arrested them?
> Where do they take them?

> IMAN
>
> Why does Rezvan have such friends?

> NAJMEH
>
> My dear, she can't do an entry test for making friends. They met at the university and became close. The poor girl didn't do anything at all.

> IMAN
>
> anyone who is arrested, and their family says that they didn't do anything.

> NAJMEH

My dear, I am telling you. This girl truly hasn't done anything.
She's been pushed into the crowd.

                    IMAN

    It is enough that she got arrested at a gathering.

                    NAJMEH

Now, can't you get any news about this child and relieve her
                    family from worry?

                    IMAN
        How do I do that? God knows where she is now.
                    They have to wait.

                    NAJMEH

                    For how long?

                    IMAN

Until she starts talking. They keep her in solitary until she
    sits in front of the camera and confesses everything.

                    NAJMEH

            What to say when she didn't do anything?

Iman looks at Najmeh.

                    IMAN

    There is always something to confess in front of the
                    interrogators' cameras.

Najmeh thinks for a while.

                    NAJMEH

            Does that mean you can't do anything?

                    IMAN

                    At this stage, no.

37. INT. LIVING ROOM- NIGHT

Iman, Najmeh, Rezvan, and Sana are sitting around the dinner table and having dinner. The TV is on and broadcasts government propaganda. Rezvan says something under her breath.

REZVAN

suffocating us with lies, turn it off, for God's sake.

Iman notices Rezvan's protest.

IMAN

what did you say dear?

REZVAN

I asked if we could turn it off while eating dinner.

IMAN

No, you said one more thing before that.

REZVAN

I said they are lying all the time.

Najmeh says under her breath "God have mercy". Iman is taken aback by the fact that Rezvan says this openly in front of him. He stops eating and tries to be cool and calm.

IMAN

Do you know all the facts?

REZVAN

I live in this country, I can see.

IMAN

what do you see? What the enemy wants? Don't you think these ideas are being fed to you?

REZVAN

Which enemy Dad? They beat my friends right in front of my eyes and arrested them.

IMAN

Wait, I agree there are some flaws. But the main point is that you and people like you don't know that the world is united against us! These are all the enemy's conspiracies.

REZVAN

Dad, what do I have to do with the unity of the world? What do I have to do with the enemy? A young girl my age was killed because of her hijab. Why?

IMAN

This! Your information is wrong, she was not killed, she had a stroke. But the enemy makes you think that she has been killed!

REZVAN

So why don't they let the issue be investigated openly? Why don't they let an independent fact-finding committee intervene? Are they killing so many people just to say they didn't kill that one person?

IMAN

Wait, you're going too far. I have been serving this system for twenty years. Me, and thousands like me are trying to protect this country from dawn to dusk, for whom? For you! Then you defend a series of thugs whose problem is getting naked in public?

REZVAN

Who wants to get naked? When did I defend getting naked?

IMAN

Those who are now in the streets.

REZVAN

Who are they, Dad? I happened to be in one of these protests yesterday. My friend Sadaf and I were coming back from university, and out of nowhere, they shot her with metal pellets in the face. Then they raided her dormitory and arrested her. Even if she survives, she'll definitely lose sight of one of her eyes. They took away the beauty of her face, her future is destroyed, why?

IMAN

I'm the one who is interrogating them day and night in the prosecutor's office and sending them to court. I know where each of them is connected to. Now you want to explain it to me?

REZVAN

Where are they connected to? Ordinary people who want an ordinary life! You've closed your eyes on reality...

NAJMEH

Enough, don't argue with your father like that, have some respect.

IMAN

Not even as a father, but as someone who has been working in this system every day as long as you lived, don't I know what's going on better than you?

REZVAN

No, because you're devoted to this system, you believe in it. You don't see its flaws.

Iman bangs on the table and gets up to leave.

IMAN

Enough, what's going on in this house?

Najmeh gets up and stops Iman from leaving.

NAJMEH

Relax, my dear... sit down. Sit down.

Najmeh pours a glass of water. She talks to Rezvan with a scolding tone.

NAJMEH

After all this time, we wanted to have dinner together just for one night, you ruined it for everyone.

Najmeh passes the glass of water to Iman. Rezvan leaves the table and goes away. Sana is sitting silently. Her eyes are filled with sadness and rage.

38. INT. NAJMEH'S BEDROOM TO LIVING ROOM- MIDNIGHT

Najmeh and Iman are sleeping on the bed. Najmeh gets up and wakes up Iman.

NAJMEH

Iman, Iman… Iman!

IMAN

hmm?

NAJMEH

You were having a dream?

IMAN

Yeah, yeah. I was dreaming.

Iman sits on the bed now. Najmeh passes him a glass of water that is on top of the drawer next to him.

NAJMEH

drink some water.

Iman drinks, then gets up and leaves the room. Najmeh is pensive.

Livingroom.

Leaning his hands on the glass of the tall window, Iman looks out. After some time, Najmeh joins him. The sound of Iman's breath can be heard.

NAJMEH

are you okay?

IMAN

I'm fine.

                    NAJMEH

            what did you dream about?

Iman doesn't respond. He is still breathing heavily.

                    NAJMEH

         Shall I bring you some sugar water?

                     IMAN

            No... I'm fine. go back to sleep.

                    NAJMEH

                  you come too.

                     IMAN

             I'll join you in a minute.

39. INT. APT- DAY (EARLY MORNING)

Bathroom.

Iman is taking a shower.

bedroom.

Najmeh is on the bed. Iman gets dressed to go to work. He wears his jacket. He opens the drawer to take his gun, but the gun is not in its place. Surprised, Iman opens the other drawer, but it is not there either. He mulls it over. He comes to the bed and softly calls Najmeh.

                     IMAN

                Najmeh, Najmeh…

Najmeh opens her eyes, but it's as if she hasn't woken up yet.

                    NAJMEH

                  Yes, darling?

> IMAN
>
> Where did you put my gun?

> NAJMEH
>
> your gun?

Iman nods.

> NAJMEH
>
> I don't know, I didn't touch your gun.

Najmeh gets up and sits on the bed.

> IMAN
>
> It's missing, the gun is missing.

Iman rushes out of the room.

Living room.

Iman looks around. He cautiously checks the apartment's entrance, making sure the door is locked. He puts his key in his pocket. Najmeh comes out of the room. Confused and shocked, she is looking at Iman. Iman is focused on scanning the apartment. He checks the windows to make sure no one has entered the apartment through the windows. Najmeh goes to the bathroom. Iman controls the place where she left the gun earlier but doesn't find anything. He then goes to the kids' bedroom. Najmeh follows him.

Girls' bedroom.

Iman slowly opens the door and enters the room. Najmeh follows him. The kids are sleeping. Iman checks the wardrobe. He looks under the bed. There is no one in the room but the kids. Iman and Najmeh return to their room.

Najmeh's bedroom.

After a short pause, Iman empties all the drawers and even checks the drawer's frame. He doesn't find anything. He's desperate.

IMAN

Maybe the kids took it, would you ask them?

NAJMEH

the kids?

IMAN

Yes, ask and find out if they took the gun.

NAJMEH

Are you sure you brought it home with you?

IMAN

Of course, I am sure.

NAJMEH

Because I didn't tell you, but that night when you weren't feeling well, you left the gun in the bathroom. I went to pick up the laundry and I saw it there. Then I picked it up and put it in the drawer.

Iman ponders for a bit.

IMAN

Last night you were standing there by the window, I came to the room. I took off my jacket. Before sitting here on the edge of the bed, I put the gun in the drawer, then I sat down.

They both pause for a moment.

IMAN

It is probably the kids, go ask them.

NAJMEH

I don't know what to ask. How should I ask?

IMAN

Just wake them up and see if they took it.

                    NAJMEH

            Ask them did you see Dad's gun?

                     IMAN

                  Yes, exactly.

Najmeh hesitates. Iman suddenly shouts.

                     IMAN

                      Go.

Shocked by Iman's behavior, Najmeh goes to the kids' bedroom.

Girls' room.

Najmeh enters the room. she softly wakes up Rezvan.

                    NAJMEH

             Rezvan... Rezvan. Dear…

                    REZVAN

                     Hmm...

                    NAJMEH

  Sweety… sweety wake up. I have to ask something important.

Rezvan wakes up.

                    REZVAN

                what's wrong, Mom?

Najmeh is fazed by the irrelevant question she's about to ask.

                    NAJMEH

 My darling, your dad's gun is missing. do you know where it is?

Rezvan gulps. Baffled, she gets up.

                    REZVAN

             A gun? Does Dad have a gun?

Najmeh doesn't know what to say.

>   NAJMEH
>
> Go back to sleep. I will explain it to you later.

Desperate, Najmeh stays there for a while. She then leaves the room without waking up Sana.

Najmeh's bedroom.

Najmeh enters the room. Iman is restless.

>   IMAN
>
> what happened?
>
>   NAJMEH
>
> I told you. The kid is frightened. They didn't even know you had a gun. Go to the prosecutor's office, maybe you don't remember and you left it there.

Iman is now doubtful. He thinks it over, then takes his bag and leaves the apartment in a hurry.

40. INT. APT. GIRLS' BEDROOM- DAY

Najmeh, Rezvan, and Sana are sitting quietly around the table. Rezvan and Sana are still in their pajamas. It seems to have just woken up. They're all silent and pensive.

41. INT./EXT. QADERI'S CAR- DAY

Qaderi's car is parked in a corner of the courthouse parking lot. In the semi-dark space, Iman and Qaderi are talking in the car.

>   QADERI
>
> Six months to three years of prison!

Iman looks at him.

                              QADERI

    Now, the prison sentence aside, the main issue is your
    professional credibility. It hasn't even been two weeks since
    you came here. It's a disgrace! All the gossip! They'll say he
           couldn't manage to keep a gun for two weeks.

Iman is agitated.

                              QADERI

    Your competence will be questioned. They'll become skeptical
         about you and get in the way of your promotion.

                               IMAN

                   I will find it no matter what.

Qaderi nods.

                              QADERI

    For now, neither report it nor talk about it with anyone.

Iman nods her head.

                              QADERI

    Based on what you say, I have no doubt that the gun is still in
      the house. Maybe if you don't do anything for a few days, the
                    one who took it brings it back.

Iman approves.

42. EXT. PROSECUTOR'S OFFICE- DAY

Iman is smoking in the yard. Two female prisoners, blindfolded, pass by him, guided by two soldiers and a female agent. Iman's phone rings.

Submission corridor.

Iman is talking on the phone while passing through the submission corridor.

                            IMAN

    No, no, Najmeh, I am sure that it's at home, probably Rezvan
          took it. Think of what she was saying last night.

43. INT. APT- DAY

Living room.

Dressed to go out, Rezvan and Sana are checking the shopping
list with Najmeh on their phone's note.

                            SANA

    Fruit, mutton, one kilo of minced meat, one and a half kilo of
         backstrap, breadcrumbs, fresh herbs, vegetables, salad
                ingredients. Walnuts, olives, and garlic.

                            NAJMEH

                Add turmeric and black pepper.

Sana adds them to the list. Najmeh gives her debit card to
Rezvan. Rezvan looks tired and sluggish. They leave the house.
As soon as they do, Najmeh rushes to the girls' bedroom.

Girls' bedroom.

Najmeh quickly and carefully searches the kids' room and their
belongings.

44. INT./EXT. IMAN'S CAR- NIGHT

Iman is driving. The car passes through a city tunnel. The
tunnel lights shine on Iman's face, and in a regular rhythm
darken and brighten his face. Iman is deep in his thoughts.

45. INT. APT. NAJMEH'S BEDROOM- NIGHT

Iman opens the drawer, but the weapon is not there. He closes
the drawer and sits on the edge of the bed. He stares at a
corner. Najmeh enters the room holding a tray and cups of tea.
She puts the tray on top of the drawer and sits next to Iman.

> IMAN
>
> I feel unsafe in my own home.
>
> NAJMEH
>
> My dear, this kind of stuff happens in all families, be patient. We'll find it.
>
> IMAN
>
> Twenty years of honest and unquestionable service is ruined overnight. All my professional reputation…
>
> NAJMEH
>
> My dear, can you lose your reputation over something that is not even your fault? You're worried for nothing.

46. INT. APT- DAY

kitchen.

Najmeh is nervously doing the dishes and rinsing them. She then cleans the sink. Suddenly, she starts thinking. She doesn't feel well.

Girls' bedroom.

The kids are lying down on the same bed, watching a video about solitary confinement on their cell phones… Suddenly, Najmeh enters.

> NAJMEH
>
> One of you took it, am I right?

Sana and Rezvan are surprised by their mother's impulsive reaction. They stare at her.

> NAJMEH
>
> Your father is about to have a stroke. If something happens to him, it's your fault!

                    REZVAN

what happened Mom? Until a few days ago, it was no one's fault
that thousands of people had strokes every day. A stroke was
just a stroke. Now today if Dad has a stroke, it is our fault?

                    NAJMEH

You have no shame...I came here to say you are playing with his
professional reputation of twenty years. You are dishonoring
him. If this gun is not found, your father should go to prison
                    for three years!

                    SANA

Mom, why do you think we took it? Do you think it's okay if I do
           the same to you and blame you for it?

Najmeh leaves the room.

47. INT. APT- NIGHT

Living room.

Rezvan and Sana are eating at the table. Najmeh is sitting far
away on the sofa, holding a cushion in her arms and watching TV.
Rezvan puts some food on a plate and takes it to Najmeh.

                    REZVAN

          Mom, come on, eat something.

Najmeh shakes her head.

                    NAJMEH

              I don't want to.

                    REZVAN

                    Why?

Rezvan sits next to Najmeh.

                    NAJMEH
You do not understand what you two are doing to your father. If,
like me, you grew up with an irresponsible father whose only

concern was gambling and having fun, you would now kiss your father's feet once a day. You wouldn't let him feel the slightest discomfort.

							REZVAN

Mom, I understand that you had a rough childhood, but that is no reason to think that everything Dad says is true. Why would Sana and I take Dad's gun?

							NAJMEH

So, the gun just vanished into thin air?

							SANA

What if Dad is lying, did you see him bring the gun home with your own eyes?

							REZVAN

You say that the gun was in the drawer, next to Dad's side of the bed. Who dares to come and take the gun from your drawer when you two are sleeping there?

							SANA

There was no weapon, Dad is so busy he got confused. He gave away his gun somewhere else and prefers to say that someone took it at home.

Najmeh is thinking.

48. EXT. PROSECUTOR'S OFFICE. YARD- DAY

Iman and Qaderi are smoking in their usual spot in the yard.

							QADERI

Your mistake was telling your wife and children what your job is.

							IMAN

Is it possible not to?

QADERI

Yes, it is.

IMAN

For how long?

QADERI

Till you're in the grave!

Iman pauses.

IMAN

I'm stuck, I don't know what to do.

QADERI

It's only natural. They don't teach us in any university or classroom how an investigating judge should interrogate his wife and children!

Iman pauses.

IMAN

I'm confused.

QADERI

Which one do you suspect the most?

IMAN

I can't believe that my children did this.

QADERI

Do you think it's your wife?

IMAN

No, I trust her completely.

Qaderi pauses for a moment.

QADERI

Really?

IMAN

Right now, I'm suspicious about everyone and everything.

QADERI

How can you live with doubts? Being afraid in your own house? There is a way that makes it easier. At least you understand how much you can trust your wife and children...

IMAN

what way?

QADERI

Alireza, take them to Alireza.

IMAN

Alireza?

QADERI

Yes, he studied for this. You know that in interrogation he is the best. He can use psychological interrogation techniques and tell you for certain who did it.

Iman takes a drag of his cigarette.

IMAN

How though? Alireza is my friend, he has been to our home many times. We've been to their place. His wife is friends with my wife. His children are friends with my children. How can I ask him to interrogate them now?

QADERI

What is an interrogation? He asks a few questions, using psychological techniques and studying their body language, and then he tells you who has the gun! What's wrong with that? Do you want everyone to find out what happened to the gun first? End this story quietly.

                              IMAN

              I can't take them to Alireza.

                             QADERI

     Do you have a safer person? Do you know a better way?

Iman stays silent and thinks it over.

49. INT. APT. LIVING ROOM- NIGHT

In the middle of the night, Najmeh and Iman are sitting far from
the TV. The TV is on.

                             NAJMEH

     Alireza and Faati are our friends, I don't want them to know
              about our family issues and private problems.

                              IMAN

          I asked Alireza not to say anything to his wife.

                             NAJMEH

       Iman, they are a married couple, they tell each other
     everything. Worse than that, do you want your children to be
                       interrogated by your friend?

                              IMAN

                They won't even know it's Alireza.

                             NAJMEH

       Who can these children trust in the future? you? me? their
                               friends?

                              IMAN

What do you suggest I should do then? Who can I trust? Can't you
see I'm stuck? This house is poisoned with mistrust. Do you know
what will happen if anyone finds out in the prosecutor's office?
Do you know what will happen if they say that his children or
                his wife have stolen his weapon?

Najmeh stays silent.

                              IMAN

      We go to Alireza's office for half an hour, he asks a few
        questions and then tells us what he thinks. He is an expert in
                                this.

Najmeh is restless. Iman takes her hands. They look into each
other's eyes.

                              NAJMEH

                      Will they record it?

                              IMAN

                       Record it for what?

                              NAJMEH

      You said yourself that they record the interrogations.

                              IMAN

                  No, there is no need to record it.

Najmeh hangs her head and gives in.

                              NAJMEH

                    I'm worried about this family.

                              IMAN

      If I go to jail, what will happen to this family? Let's fix it.

50.   EXT. IN FRONT OF THE SAFE HOUSE- DAY

Iman's car enters an alley and then stops at a corner. Najmeh,
Rezvan, and Sana get out of the car. They go to a house nearby.
Najmeh rings the doorbell. While sitting in the driver's seat,
Iman looks at them waiting in front of the door. Sana looks at
the CCTV camera which its angle of view is set on the entrance
door. Rezvan is looking at her father in the car. The door
opens. Rezvan and Sana enter. Najmeh looks at Iman before
entering. Iman nods.

51. INT. SAFE HOUSE- DAY

The entrance of the building to the hall.

Sana, Rezvan, and Najmeh pass through an x-ray screening device. A hijabed woman guides them inside. It seems the house tries to look like a place of living in a tasteless manner. Upon reaching the hall, the woman asks Rezvan, Sana, and Najameh to sit there and wait.

                    FEMALE AGENT

              Sit here, I'll be back.

Rezvan nervously looks at Najmeh. But for Sana, everything seems to be normal. It is as if she has come to a doctor's office. A little later, the female agent comes to the hall and asks Sana and Rezvan to follow her. Rezvan looks at her mother again. With a nod, Najmeh asks her to follow the woman. Najmeh remains alone. Alireza comes a little later.

                    ALIREZA

                    Hello.

                    NAJMEH

       Hello sir, how are you? How is dear Faati?

                    ALIREZA

       Thank you very much. Can I take a moment of your time?

Najmeh, who is confused, doesn't know what to say.

                    NAJMEH

          Are you going to talk to me too?

                    ALIREZA

              Just a few questions.

                    NAJMEH

      Iman said you are only going to talk to the kids.

Alireza is now speaking in a commanding tone.

ALIREZA

Please, come this way.

Reluctantly, Najmeh follows the way Alireza is showing to her.

Interrogation room.

There is nothing in the interrogation room except for two chairs with armrests. One of the two chairs is facing the wall. As soon as he enters, Alireza turns it around and places it in front of the other chair.

ALIREZA

please have a seat.

Najmeh and Alireza sit on each chair.

ALIREZA

You must know that I am here at your service due to Iman's request so that we can solve this problem with each other's help.

NAJMEH

yes, yes, I know.

ALIREZA

I generally do not mix professional issues and friendship, but sometimes friends have to help each other out.

NAJMEH

I'm very grateful. Thank you.

Alireza is observing Najmeh. He monitors the way she sits, her hands, and her eyes.

Alireza starts writing on the paper in front of him.

ALIREZA

I ask you to please patiently and carefully, answer the questions that I am writing.

NAJMEH

Honestly, I think it is very unlikely that the kids took the gun.

Alireza responds with a laugh.

ALIREZA

Usually, the culprit is someone who we can think of the least!

NAJMEH

It's not even about a crime. Iman has lost his gun somewhere else. You yourself know these days' conditions better. You are all busy, and under pressure. Iman is very nervous too. Especially in the last few days, he had written several death penalty sentences, which mentally had a great impact on him.

ALIREZA

I understand. But Iman is sure that he brought the gun home and put it in its usual place.

NAJMEH

I know, he told me too.

ALIREZA

You know the impact of a lost gun on Iman's career path.

NAJMEH

Of course, I know, but it is not okay that he insists the gun is missing in the house and that he suspects the kids took it. This really bothers me.

ALIREZA

What about you?

NAJMEH

What about me?

ALIREZA

It is not possible that you yourself know where the gun is?

                              NAJMEH

          what do you mean? You mean I took his gun?

                              ALIREZA

            Anyway, in my job, this is a possibility.

                              NAJMEH

        Wow, thank you for that… and many thanks to Iman…

                              ALIREZA

    No, no, Iman told me that he trusts you one hundred percent.
      Please don't be upset. You know better that sometimes there are
                  secrets between children and their mothers.

                              NAJMEH

    There is no such thing at all. If I know something, why should I
      hide it from my husband? In the past twenty-two years, I have
             always been completely transparent and honest with Iman.

                              ALIREZA

    But I know there are some cases that Iman does not know about.

    Najmeh thinks for a moment and suddenly, decides to leave. She
    gets up.

                              ALIREZA

                         Please sit down.

                              NAJMEH

                  No, your words are insulting.

                              ALIREZA

    Please, I am talking to you with the utmost respect. This room
      has never seen such respect for the person who sits in that
      chair. I assure you; whatever is said between us, won't leave
      this room. I'm your confidant. I just wanted to say that this
      case can be similar to the issue you didn't want to tell Iman
                           for some reason.

    With her silence, Najmeh conveys that she's displeased.

                              NAJMEH

You're saying I don't understand the disaster that is happening?

                              ALIREZA

      It is important to tell me everything you know.

With the look on her face, it is obvious that Najmeh has
surrendered to Alireza's wishes.

The other interrogation room.

This room is similar to the other room, only smaller. There are
only two chairs with armrests. A chair is facing the wall and
Rezvan is sitting on it. For a long time, Rezvan has been
staring at the wall without moving. She starts to read the
writings on the wall. *Salvation lies in honesty, God help me.
Mother, forgive me...* suddenly the female agent enters with a
blindfold in her hand.

                           FEMALE AGENT

         Don't turn around... cover your eyes with this.

Rezvan takes the blindfold and puts it over her eyes.

                           FEMALE AGENT

     Pull it up a bit, so you can see in front of you. So you can
                         write on the paper.

Rezvan does as the agent asks.

                           FEMALE AGENT

                  Don't move until I come back.

For a few moments, Rezvan remains alone. She does not move on
the officer's command. A little later, the female agent returns.
After controlling the blindfolds and making sure Rezvan can't
see anything, she points to Alireza to enter. Alireza enters and
sits on a chair. He starts writing some questions on a piece of
paper.

Alireza writes: "Introduce yourself thoroughly".

Alireza puts the paper along with the pen on the chair in front
    of Rezvan. Rezvan takes the pen and starts writing. Alireza

stares at Rezvan's movements. A little later, Rezvan holds the paper behind her head. Alireza takes the paper. He takes a short time to read the paper, but then stares at Rezvan once more. A little later, Alireza starts writing again.

Alireza writes: "Explain fully and precisely where you were and what you were doing when the weapon went missing".

Alireza puts the paper in front of Rezvan and Rezvan starts writing. Alireza is staring at her.

The other interrogation room.

This time it is Sana who is holding the piece of paper behind her head. Alireza takes the paper from her and takes a look at her answer. Then he watches Sana and her behavior. A little later he starts writing. He puts the paper in front of Sana. From Sana's point of view, we see the Alireza's hands. As he places the paper in front of Sana, we see that he is wearing a unique agate ring on his finger. Seeing the ring, Sana pauses a little and then starts writing.

52. INT./EXT. IMAN'S CAR. TEHRAN'S STREETS- DAY

Iman, Najmeh, Rezvan, and Sana are in the car, driving in the streets of Tehran towards home. The girls are sitting in the back seat, quiet and disheartened. Najmeh is distraught and Iman is lost in his thoughts. He looks at Rezvan in the mirror for a few moments. Rezvan is staring out the window. Najmeh and Iman exchange a glance.

53. INT. APT- NIGHT

Living room.

Rezvan and Sana are sitting on the sofa. Iman and Najmeh are standing. Something like a court has been staged. Najmeh is speaking to Sana.

NAJMEH

You go to the room.

IMAN

Stay. There is nothing to hide.

Rezvan is staring ahead.

        REZVAN

    I have nothing to say.

        NAJMEH

  Do you understand what you are doing?

        REZVAN

     what am I doing?

        NAJMEH

You are playing with your father's 20-year reputation, with the fate of the family.

        IMAN

My dear daughter, this will affect my professional records, they will put me in jail.

        REZVAN

   What does it have to do with me?

Iman tries to stay calm.

        IMAN

My dear, sometimes you do something exciting that with the passage of time you realize is wrong. But fear does not allow one to go back and admit their mistakes. But I want to assure you that you should not be afraid. Something has happened, and now we have to fix it. That's it. Just hand over the gun and everything will be over.

        REZVAN

Which gun, dad? Why don't you believe that I don't know anything about it? Does that mean you are ready to accuse me because of the words of a stranger?

        NAJMEH

So what happened to this gun? It just disappeared? where is it?

                          REZVAN

I do not know. How do we know that you didn't get it yourself,
                            Mom?

                          NAJMEH

                   I will smack you so...

                           IMAN

   Najmeh! Dear Rezvan, the expert evaluated Mom's behavior as
               well. Now, calm down, my dear.

Iman sits in front of Rezvan.

                           IMAN

   My darling, look into my eyes. I'm your father. I worked
  honestly for years, and now the result of all those years is
  being destroyed. I will go to prison. do you want to hurt me?
  Why? Did you see anything but love and support from me? The best
     house, the best life...car, money. What else do you want?

Tears roll in Iman's eyes. Rezvan bursts into tears from the
pressure, and while crying profusely, she defends herself.

                          REZVAN

    I didn't take it, I swear. I didn't take it, I swear on my
   grandmother's grave, I didn't even know that Dad had a gun. I
           didn't take it, let me go. let me go...

Facing Rezvan's tears, Iman sits on the sofa. Najmeh angrily
rushes to the girls' bedroom.

Girls' bedroom.

As soon as Najmeh enters the room, she starts searching the room
with anger. She throws everything around in search of the gun.
Sana goes toward her, to calm her down.

                           SANA

                   Mom, what are you doing?

                          NAJMEH

             No matter what, I will find this gun.

Iman comes to the room and hugs Najmeh. Najmeh calms down a bit, but suddenly pushes Iman aside and starts speaking to Sana.

NAJMEH

hasn't she told you anything?

SANA

Mom, do you want to pick on me now?

NAJMEH

Didn't you want to dye your hair blue? Your father is here, he promises to let you dye your hair blue. Tell her Iman, tell her you allow her to do so.

IMAN

Yes, dear. I allow it. You can dye your hair and paint your nails. If you know anything, tell us. Look, Rezvan is not doing well now. She will thank you later.

Sana looks at them with disdain.

SANA

she didn't tell me anything.

Sana leaves the room. Najmeh and Iman are desperate.

54. INT. APT- MIDNIGHT

Living room.

In the dark, Iman is sitting near the window, facing the city, and listening to the sound of a prayer on his phone. Near him, Najmeh is sitting on the ground wearing a chador and muttering a prayer. The prayer ends. They sit in silence for a while.

IMAN

Where did we go wrong?

NAJMEH

Maybe this child is truly innocent.

IMAN

No, something's going on.

NAJMEH

What?

IMAN

They are hiding something.

NAJMEH

How are you so sure?

IMAN

Sana knows something... the look on her face said she knows something.

NAJMEH

Iman Sana is just a kid. This is your house, not the courthouse. don't look at them like criminals.

Iman looks at Najmeh.

NAJMEH

Whatever has happened was only a mistake. You said it yourself, the bridges behind them should not be destroyed.

IMAN

I feel that even the walls of this house are lying to me.

NAJMEH

Why? Whatever happens, you have your family in the end.

IMAN

I'm humiliated; I look helpless.

NAJMEH

says who?

IMAN

You know better than anyone that I came from the lowest social class, without any acquaintances or help, I was able to reach here only with personal effort and honesty.

NAJMEH

Everyone knows this.

Iman is fighting back his tears. Najmeh takes Iman's hands.

NAJMEH

Oh my dear, relax. Everything's gonna be alright. Everything will be fine.

IMAN

I want to hug Rezvan and Sana.

NAJMEH

Then go to their room and hug them.

IMAN

No, no, I can't do it now. I want to think and figure out where I went wrong.

NAJMEH

What do you mean?

IMAN

Why does Sana want to dye her hair at this age? blue! Why does She like to paint her nails?

NAJMEH

My dear, the world has changed, young people think differently.

IMAN

The world has changed, but God hasn't changed. God's rules have not changed.

                    NAJMEH

          This should be taught to them.

                     IMAN

      Didn't I tell them these things up till now?

                    NAJMEH

   Sure, you did. but now at this age, they are influenced by their
                       classmates, friends…

                     IMAN

        She shouldn't be friends with such people.

                    NAJMEH

   You should spend more time at home. Get close to them. Shape
                         their mindset.

Iman thinks about it. He nods in agreement.

Najmeh's bedroom.

In bed, Iman and Najmeh are making love.

55. INT. APT- DAY

kitchen.

Najmeh is doing the dishes in the kitchen. She is repeating a prayer under her breath. Sana rushes out of the room.

                     SANA

                   Mom... Mom.

By raising her voice, Najmeh tells Sana that she cannot speak. Despite all this, Sana keeps her phone screen in front of Najmeh's face. After a few moments, Najmeh suddenly becomes silent. She turns off the tap and takes the phone from Sana.

                    NAJMEH

                  what is this?

                              SANA

It's on the internet. It's the father's information, they wrote
                  the home address as well.

                             NAJMEH

                         Oh God, oh Lord.

56. INT. PROSECUTOR'S OFFICE- DAY

Submission corridor.

Iman walks towards Qaderi's office with quick steps while
passing through the submission corridor.

Qaderi's office.

Iman enters Qaderi's room. Seeing Iman, Qaderi gets up. He hands
him a few prints of images from social media pages. Iman looks
at the papers. The corporate photo ID, his name and surname,
along with some other details can be seen on the paper under the
phrase "Identified". Seeing this, Iman is enraged. He sits on a
chair.

                              IMAN

  Someone is behind this story. Someone wants to get rid of me.

                             QADERI

                   I told you to be careful.

Iman looks at him desperately.

                             QADERI

              It's time to report the missing gun.

Behind his desk, Qaderi goes toward a metal filing cabinet in
the corner of the room. He opens a drawer and pulls out some
files.

                             QADERI

Take this situation seriously. Write a letter to the head of the
      prosecutor's office right now. explain that your private

> information has been leaked in cyberspace, and you are in danger. Request an institutional home with high-level security in a safe area. Take this letter to the president's office, register it, and go back home quickly. Take your wife and children and go to a safe place for a few days until things clear out.

Qaderi takes out a gun from among the files. He puts it on the table in front of Iman.

> QADERI
>
> I have two, this one can stay with you for now.

Iman looks at the gun. He takes deep breaths out of desperation. He feels helpless.

> QADERI
>
> What are you waiting for?

Iman gets up, takes the gun, and puts it under his jacket. He hugs Qaderi and leaves the room.

57. INT./EXT. IMAN'S CAR. STREET TO APARTMENT- DAY

Streets.

Iman rushes through the streets towards home while wearing a mask. He is constantly scanning his surroundings by looking around and in the mirror. He feels like he's being followed. At an intersection (that we've seen at the beginning of the movie) he stops at a red light. A car pulls up next to him. For a moment, he makes eye contact with the driver of this car. The driver is a woman who stares into the eyes of Iman. Iman is frightened by the woman's piercing glance. He drives on.

In front of the building's parking lot.

Iman arrives home. Near the entrance of the parking lot, a motorcyclist has parked his motorcycle and is waiting. Although Iman keeps an eye on the motorcyclist, he tries to seem indifferent towards him. After entering the parking lot and parking his car, Iman hides in a corner and watches the motorcyclist. Now the motorcyclist is talking on the phone. Iman rushes to the elevator.

the apartment. Living room.

Without paying attention to anything, Iman enters the apartment and goes to the bedroom. Najmeh is in the kitchen. She is surprised by Iman's behavior.

Najmeh's bedroom.

Iman observes the motorcyclist from the bedroom's window. The motorcyclist gets out of his sight. Iman starts to change his clothes but suddenly the doorbell rings. Iman rushes out of the room and toward the doorbell camera.

Living room.

Surprised, Najmeh stops working and looks at him. Iman answers the door.

IMAN

Yes, yes ...

Najmeh is stunned, she approaches Iman.

IMAN

who is it?

NAJMEH

My dear, no one rang the doorbell.

Iman looks at Najmeh in shock. After a short pause, he hangs up. He goes to the entrance door and looks out through the peephole. He locks the entrance door and puts the key in his pocket. He goes to the bedroom.

Najmeh's bedroom.

Najmeh follows Iman to the bedroom.

NAJMEH

Are you alright honey?

IMAN

Yeah, yeah, I'm fine.

                              NAJMEH

                    what are you worried about?

Iman looks at Najmeh.

                               IMAN

                        where is your phone?

Najmeh takes out her phone from her pocket. Iman takes it and
gets up. He goes to the kids' bedroom and enters.

Sana and Rezvan are surprised.

                               SANA

                            Hello Dad.

                              REZVAN

                              Hello.

                               IMAN

                        Hello, your phones?

The girls are surprised. Both hand over their phones. From their
desk drawer, Iman takes paper stickers and a marker. He puts a
note on each phone and writes the owner's name. Iman asks
Rezvan.

                               IMAN

                         Phone's password?

Rezvan is surprised by his father's behavior and answers after a
pause.

                              REZVAN

                      Two thousand and three.

Iman writes the pin on the sticker and then sticks another one
on the phone's camera.

                               IMAN

                              Sana...

Sana hesitates to answer.

SANA

Give me the phone.

Iman gives back Sana's phone. Sana draws a pattern on the points that appear on the screen. The phone opens. Iman takes the phone back and draws the same pattern on the paper tape. He also sticks a piece of tape on the phone's camera.

IMAN

Najmeh, your phone password?

After a short pause, Najmeh answers.

NAJMEH

the same as you had.

IMAN

Be at the table in five minutes, I want to talk.

Iman leaves the room with the phones.

Living room.

Sana, Rezvan, Najmeh, and Iman are sitting around the table. Iman speaks and other family members listen.

IMAN

Until today, I tried my best to provide for your comfort and peace. But now I am worried about this situation. Strange things have been happening for a while. We are all tired and we don't want these bad incidents to continue. We will leave Tehran for a few days. We are going to my father's house. You have loved that place since you were a child, but I haven't had a chance to take you there in a few years. Now is a good time. We are going to be the family we used to be again. For now, phones stay with me. In these few days, we stay away from news and events and instead try to solve our problems. We will leave in an hour.

58. INT./EXT. STREETS OF TEHRAN TO THE OUTSKIRTS OF THE CITY- DAY (BEFORE NOON)

Streets of Tehran.

Najmeh, Sana, Rezvan, and Iman are in the car, driving through the streets of Tehran and getting out of the city.

Desert highway.

The car is driving fast on the desert highway.

59. INT./EXT. GAS STATION TO DESERT. DAY (AFTERNOON)

At a gas station on the road, Iman is refueling the car. He suddenly feels that the two passengers in the car behind them in the line are staring at him and talking about him. Iman looks away, facing the opposite direction. A little later, he turns his gaze to the car to make sure that the situation is safe. As he looks back, the young woman who is sitting in the passenger seat suddenly lowers her phone (which is filming). Seeing this, Iman is startled. He quickly finishes refueling and after paying, gets into his car without showing any reaction. After getting into the car, he sees in the mirror that they are filming and taking pictures of his car. Rezvan and Sana are sleeping in the back seat. But Najmeh notices the change in Iman's state. Iman starts the car and slowly leaves the gas station.

NAJMEH

Has something happened?

IMAN

No.

Najmeh looks behind her.

NAJMEH

I can tell by your state, did they recognize you?

Najmeh tries again to see the reaction of the passengers in the car behind them.

IMAN

Do not turn around.

NAJMEH

what has happened?

Rezvan wakes up.

IMAN

They were filming us and taking photos.

Najmeh takes a mask towards Iman and hands a few masks to the back seat.

NAJMEH

put on your mask. Guys, wear a mask.

Sana wakes up.

SANA

What's going on?

REZVAN

Here, wear a mask. While he was filling in the gas, a guy took photos and videos of him and the car.

Iman stops at a corner.

NAJMEH

Iman let's go. Please, didn't you say let's do something to end the problems?

IMAN

I will not allow anyone to harm me and my family.

Iman has parked his car in a corner and is waiting for the other car to come out of the gas station. Now everyone is wearing a mask. Rezvan looks behind her. The car is still in the station.

NAJMEH

I swear on your father's grave, let it go.

                          REZVAN

    Dad, come on. Let's go. We're not in the mood for another
                          conflict.

Sana looks around silently. Iman watches the car leaving the gas
station in the side mirror. The other car passes by without
noticing Iman's car. Iman waits for a while, then comes out of
the parking spot. It enters the main road. Iman increases his
speed. Now it is at a proper distance from that car, and he
tries to maintain this distance. Iman turns to Najmeh and points
at the glove box.

                           IMAN

              Glove box. Take out your phone.

Najmeh opens the glove box and takes out her mobile phone from a
plastic bag in which all phones are kept. she turns on the
phone.

                           IMAN

   First, take a photo from the back so the license plate can be
                       seen clearly.

Najmeh does so.

                           IMAN

   I'm going to drive beside their car. I'll drive next to them;
                   you record their faces.

Iman increases the speed and suddenly changes direction and
drives parallel to the other car. In response, the driver and
passenger of the other car start filming Najmeh and Iman.

Iman looks ahead, and as soon as he sees a side road, he
suddenly turns the stirring wheel and drives towards it, trying
to force the other car onto that road.

The cars collide. With a few more hits, he now forces the other
car to deviate to the right and drive on the dirt shoulder.
After driving for some time on the dirt shoulder, the other car
tries in vain to return to the main road. It eventually has to
turn to the side road.

Missing the side road, Iman hits the brakes, reverses
immediately, and resumes the chase. Going down a path deep in

the desert, the car in front suddenly stops. Two passengers (a young man and a woman) get off and are waiting for Iman's car to arrive while they're recording with their phones. Iman reaches there and hurriedly gets out of his car.

Najmeh turns to the kids.

NAJMEH

Don't you get out of the car.

Najmeh gets out of the car as she's aiming her phone's camera towards the passengers of the other car. As soon as Najmeh gets out of the car, Iman suddenly pulls out his gun and shouts and orders them to lie down on the ground.

IMAN

Lie down on the ground, come on, quick. Drop your phones and lie down on the ground.

Inside the car.

Rezvan and Sana are shocked by seeing Iman's reaction.

REZVAN

what is Dad doing?

SANA

He still has a gun!

REZVAN

Has he gone crazy? let's take the phone and call Uncle Asad!

From between the two front seats, Sana goes toward the glove box to take out the bag of mobile phones. She takes the bag and returns to the back seat.

Outside the car.

MAN

Why are you afraid, Mr. Judge? Are you worried that your family's going to find out what your job is or know that their father is a murderer?

Iman shouts.

> IMAN
>
> Shut up, lay on the ground, quick...lay down...

Inside the car.

Phones are on. Sana and Rezvan are waiting for the network connection.

outside the car.

> WOMAN
>
> Shoot us if you can. Shoot.

The woman addresses Sana and Rezvan.

> WOMAN
>
> Girls, do you know what your father does? Do you know how many requests for death sentences have been issued by him just recently? Did you read what they wrote about him?

Sana and Rezvan have conflicting feelings. On one hand, it is a shame and on the other, it's a conflict between their family and two strangers.

> NAJMEH
>
> Shut up you bitch.

> WOMAN
>
> You're very polite too... whatever I am, I'm definitely better than you and people like you who dip your bread in people's blood. If you think I'm afraid of your husband's gun you're mistaken. Right now, I'm sending your image live online so that you can be exposed to the whole world.

Rezvan and Sana have noticed that the phones are not working. Hearing this threat, Sana screams.

> SANA
>
> She's lying mom, there's no connection here, she can't send anything.

Iman looks at Rezvan and Sana.

                         IMAN

   I'm telling you for the last time, drop your phones and lie on
                 the ground. I swear to Allah I'll shoot!

Iman's screams and threats are effective enough that the man retreats.

                         MAN

   Alright, alright. We'll do whatever you want. Stop pointing the
                          gun at us.

The man puts his phone on the ground. He turns to the woman.

                         MAN

                    Drop the phone.

Surprised by the man's reaction, the woman continues filming.

                         MAN

   Ensi Please, don't you see that he is armed? he is swearing to
    God that he is going to shoot. This guy will shoot! drop the
                          phone.

Desperate, the woman throws the phone on the ground with reluctance and anger.

                         IMAN

                        IDs...

The man takes out his wallet from his pocket and drops the ID card along with the wallet.

Iman turns to the woman.

                         IMAN

                    You...your ID?

                         WOMAN

                My bag is in the car.

IMAN

alright. Go back. Keep your distance. Go back. Lie on the ground with your hands behind your neck.

The man and the woman do whatever Iman says. Iman looks at Najmeh. Najmeh unties the shawl around the woman's neck and cuts it in two pieces, in order to tie their hands and feet. Seeing how they're treating the man and the woman, Rezvan gets angry.

REZVAN

They took their mobile phones, they can delete the videos, give them back the phones and we can leave.

Suddenly Rezvan's gaze is drawn to the car's footwell. She sees the gun.

REZVAN

Sana?

SANA

Yes, my dear?

Sana notices the direction of Rezvan's gaze. She looks at the footwell and sees the gun. She looks at Rezvan.

REZVAN

What is this? It was you?

Sana nods in approval.

REZVAN

Give it to me.

SANA

Let me keep it myself.

REZVAN

I told you to give it to me.

Sana gives the gun to Rezvan. Rezvan hurriedly and cautiously puts it in the pocket of the front seat cover.

outside the car.

Najmeh finishes binding the hands and feet of the man and the woman. They are lying face down on the ground. Iman takes their mobile phones and gives them to Rezvan.

> IMAN
>
> Turn them off. And remove their SIM cards.

Rezvan starts doing as she's been told. Iman goes toward the car. He picks up the car keys and comes near the man. He sits next to him. In front of the man's eyes, he throws the keys away with all his might. then he gets close to the man's ear.

> IMAN
>
> Find the keys before it gets dark because there are many wolves out here. Thank God that I let you live, out of respect for my wife and children. I hope it will be a lesson and you will not make such mistakes again.

Iman's car leaves the scene.

60. EXT. DESERT ROADS TP THE ORCHARD- DAY

Iman's car is driving fast on a desert road.

Iman's car is driving on a dirt side road.

Iman's car passes in front of the remains of an abandoned and uninhabited village.

After driving a short distance from the village, Iman's car stops in front of his paternal mansion which is surrounded by an orchard.

61. INT./EXT. ORCHARD TO HOUSE- DAY (ALMOST NIGHT)

Sana opens the gate. Iman's car drives in the orchard. Sana then closes the gate.

It's twilight. Sana, Rezvan, Najmeh, and Iman take their bags and suitcases from the car. Rezvan and Sana exchange a few looks. Rezvan points to Sana and insists that the gun should remain in the pocket of the seat cover of the car.

Rezvan, Sana, and Najmeh follow Iman through the dry trees to the mansion at the end of the orchard.

With a set of keys, Iman opens the mansion's entrance door. An old house that seems to have been abandoned for a long time.

Sana and Rezvan are cleaning the house.

Iman and Najmeh shake a blanket and prepare it so it can be used.

Out of a stool, a wire with a lamp attached to it, and a velvet quilt, Iman makes a Korsi (a type of low table with a heater underneath and blankets thrown over it).

62. INT. HOUSE'S LIVING ROOM- NIGHT

Iman Najmeh, Rezvan, and Sana are sitting around the Korsi. Rezvan and Sana are holding a video camera and, on its screen, they're watching old videos of a family picnic by the sea. In this video, Iman is filming family members with the same camera. Sana also is filming Iman with her phone. They seem happy. Rezvan and Sana are staring at these nostalgic images.

Iman has a prayer book in his hand and is reading. Najmeh looks at Iman.

                    NAJMEH

        Why didn't you say that the gun was found?

Iman answers without taking his eyes off the book.

                    IMAN

    It's not. This one was lent to me by Qaderi. He has two.

Najmeh sighs.

                    NAJMEH

        I was happy, I thought this nightmare was over.

This last sentence attracts Iman's attention. He takes his eyes off the book and stares at her face. The power goes out.

IMAN

I think the fuse blew. I go and reset it.

Iman gets up from around the Korsi.

63. EXT. MANSION TO ORCHARD'S ENTRANCE AND POWER BOX- NIGHT

The light of the full moon shines on the orchard. Iman comes out of the mansion. The wind is blowing. Iman walks the length of the orchard through the trees toward the power box (near the entrance to the garden). He reaches the box and resets the fuse.

64. INT./EXT. ORCHARD- DAY (EARLY MORNING)

External.

The mansion can be seen among the trees.

Internal.

In the house, Iman is preparing the breakfast table alone. Now and then he takes out something from the picnic basket.

He pours some water from a bottle of mineral water into a teapot. Steam rises from the kettle on the stove. Iman pours boiling water from the kettle into the teapot. Najmeh, Iman, Rezvan, and Sana are sitting around the breakfast table.

NAJMEH

Wow, thank you! what a breakfast!

SANA

Dad, when will you give us our phones? We're so bored here.

IMAN

Don't rush, dear. I'll give you back your phones soon.

Rezvan is silent. As if she is still upset. Iman tries to talk to her. He puts a cup of tea in front of her.

IMAN

Don't let your tea get cold, my dear.

REZVAN

Thank you.

SANA

Dad, can we see your family album on this trip?

IMAN

Family album! During our childhood, we had to go to the city to take pictures. It wasn't like now; everyone had a phone in their hands and could take a picture at any moment and quickly send it to this and that. Taking pictures had its own principle. Having an album was quite fancy.

SANA

Does that mean you don't have any photos of your parents and siblings, or your childhood?

IMAN

No, I have one.

SANA

where is it?

IMAN

It should be here, I will find it and show it to you. I was five years old. After a few years of planning and saving money, Grandpa took us to the city in Karbalaei Suleiman's van. Grandma, Aunt Zahra, Uncle Ali, and me. From there we went by train to Mashhad to visit Imam Reza's shrine. We definitely had to take pictures there. Because when we came back, everyone from the village would come to our house, and in short, it was very important for them to see our photo in the shrine of Imam Reza. On the other hand, photography was not allowed in Imam Reza's shrine. But some photographers had a large painting of the shrine, in front of which the pilgrims would stand and take pictures. We also went to one of these photo shoots and stood like this and took a photo.

Iman puts his hand on his heart. Sana jokingly mimics his gesture.

SANA

What does that mean?

IMAN

It means surrender. It means devotion. Unquestioning faith and obedience.

Sana looks at her father. Rezvan also looks at him, discreetly.

SANA

Is that what you want from us?

IMAN

I don't want it for myself, I want it for God.

SANA

Well, what do you have to do with the relationship between me and God?

NAJMEH

Sana!!!

SANA

We are talking, mom.

NAJMEH

What kind of conversation is this?

SANA

I am asking a question.

NAJMEH

Faith means not questioning everything.

                              IMAN

Faith of heart. Peace is the result of the faith of heart, but
oh the day when one loses faith in the heart… This is what
                     happened to me recently.

Iman's words and the shift in his tone change the tone of the
conversation as well.

                              IMAN
           It's terrible for a person to lose trust and
           faith of heart in his family members. He feels
             that every moment he is being humiliated by
                          hearing a lie.
           Finding a weapon is no longer a priority for me.
            I want to find the liar. Every day, our family
                is being threatened by lies and secrecy.

No one knows how to react to Iman's strange behavior.

                              IMAN

           Among the four of us, at least one is a liar.
            This person is destroying the trust between
           family members and is destroying the family with
                         lies and secrecy.

Najmeh is frightened by Iman's change of tone. Rezvan pulls
herself together. Sana listens to Iman's words without the
slightest reaction.

                              IMAN
             What is clear is that I am not a liar.
           So, it's someone among you. Assuming the gun
           thief didn't tell anyone else that she did it,
            we only have one liar. But my work experience
             says that in reality there may be up to three
                         liars in this group.

No one wants to say something against Iman's words.

                              IMAN

I'm tired. I'm angry. I am sad. And I want to leave it up to you
             to find out which one of you has the gun.

The silence caused by Iman's terrifying tone continues.

IMAN

You have one hour to talk and convince the liar to admit her mistake. I promise there will be no punishment, but the liar must make up for what happened. You have one hour!

Iman locks the entrance of the mansion from outside and leaves Rezvan, Sana, and Najmeh alone.

REZVAN

What an articulated speech!

Najmeh is absolutely disheartened.

NAJMEH

It shouldn't have come to this.

SANA

I hate his behavior.

REZVAN

Why didn't we tell him that the first liar was you who hid your job from your family for all these years?

NAJMEH

It's too late. I know your father. Whoever did this, this is the end of this game, you have to stop.

REZVAN

Mom, how can we be sure you didn't do it?

NAJMEH
You don't seem to understand what is happening.
I'm begging you, for God's sake, if you know
where this damn gun is, stop this game. Just give
it to me. I'll say I'm the thief, I'm the liar.

Rezvan uses this opportunity and points to Sana not to trust these words in any way.

SANA

Your mistake is that you never stood up to him.

                              NAJMEH

All my life, I have tried hard so that you never see this side
                         of your father.

From the window, we see Iman walking in the orchard outside the
mansion.

                              NAJMEH

      Do you want to say which one of you has the gun?

                              REZVAN

                     We don't know anything.

Najmeh looks at Sana, but she doesn't get an answer. She then
turns to Rezvan, and Rezvan has nothing more to say either.

                              NAJMEH

                   Is this your final answer?

Najmeh faces the girls' silence. After a pause, she goes to the
window. She draws Iman's attention to herself by knocking on the
window glass a few times. Iman looks at Najmeh and comes toward
the mansion.

Iman opens the door and enters.

                              IMAN

    Well, it's great that you came to a conclusion this fast.

                              NAJMEH

                  It was me... I have the gun.

Iman shows his surprise.

                              IMAN

      Ah... So, it was you? It's hard to believe... are you
sacrificing yourself for them? Are you taking the blame for one
   of the girls? Does that mean more lies on top of lies, again?

Najmeh shouts.

                            NAJMEH

I'm not lying. I hated that gun from the first night you brought
         it home, you were excited, but I was scared.

Iman looks at Najmeh and the girls for a few moments. First, he
goes to the front door calmly and locks the door. After that, he
goes to the window and picks up the video camera in silence. He
then mounts it on the tripod in front of Najmeh, closes the
frame, and starts recording the image.

                             IMAN

  So I lived with a liar for twenty years! What other lies have
                         you told me?

The sound of Najmeh's breathing can be heard. She stays silent
for a while and doesn't know what to say.

                            NAJMEH

                   I did not lie to you.

Iman shouts.

                             IMAN

                    So what game is this?

Najmeh speaks with a lump in her throat.

                            NAJMEH

                     Calm down, my dear.

Iman continues sternly.

                             IMAN

                      where is the gun?

                            NAJMEH

         I threw it in the water canal near the house.

                             IMAN

                        You are lying!

NAJMEH

I'm not lying.

IMAN

Ah, the deception of you women.
"He said, It is part of your plot. Indeed, your plot is great."

Sana and Rezvan are staring at Iman, bewildered and a little scared.

NAJMEH

I'm sorry, I made a mistake, forgive me, let's go back to Tehran, I'll show you where I dropped the gun, maybe it can still be found.

Rezvan is angry about how Iman is treating her mother.

IMAN

When and how did you steal the gun?

NAJMEH

You were moaning in your sleep in the middle of the night, I woke you up and gave you water. Then you went out in the living room. I used the opportunity and took the gun.

IMAN

After you took the gun, where did you hide it?
When and how did you throw it into the water canal?

NAJMEH

At the right moment, I put the gun in a plastic bag in the freezer, between frozen meats.

Looking at each other, Sana and Rezvan are surprised by Najmeh's answer and storytelling. Iman is staring at Najmeh's eyes. Najmeh hangs her head.

NAJMEH

When you went to work, I brought the gun, wrapped it in a piece of cloth, took it down to the iron bridge over the water canal, and threw it in.

IMAN

And didn't you think what you are doing with your husband's reputation?

NAJMEH

I was afraid.

Iman stares at Najmeh with utmost rage.

NAJMEH

Iman please, I beg you. Stop this. Let's go back to Tehran. I tell everyone that I did this, I swear I will not let it harm your job...
Let's go back to Tehran. Look at the girls, they're afraid. I will come to whatever court you say, I will admit that I took the gun. Don't be afraid, I tell everyone you did whatever you could.

Iman tries to control himself. Najmeh burst into tears. She starts crying.

IMAN

I am not afraid of anyone.

REZVAN

If you are not afraid of anyone, why do you want a gun?

NAJMEH

My dear, don't say anything. You and Sana shouldn't get involved in this.

REZVAN

We were involved in this from the beginning. Get up Mom, stand up.

Iman looks at Rezvan in surprise.

REZVAN

I have the gun. it's right here. I will call Uncle to come and take Mom and Sana, when they leave, I will give you the gun.

IMAN

So I'm faced with a family coup! Sit in front of the camera.

REZVAN

I won't.

IMAN

How dare you.

Najmeh gets up and goes to Rezvan.

NAJMEH

Dear mom, come and sit on this chair, and answer your dad's questions, please. Don't be bitter, let things calm down.

Against her will, Rezvan sits on the chair in front of the camera at her mother's request, to avoid further tension.

IMAN

Explain when and how you took the gun. What was your motivation?

REZVAN

I will not answer your questions.

IMAN

I will make you talk.

NAJMEH

Please talk to him my darling, I beg you.

REZVAN

Don't you want your gun? I have it with me, in this orchard. Let Mom and Sana go, I will give you the gun.

IMAN

When you give me the gun, we will return to Tehran.

REZVAN

I will not give back the gun until you let them go.

                                IMAN

             Don't impose conditions on me.

                               REZVAN

    You are not in a good way dad when you get better, you will be
                        ashamed of your actions.

                               NAJMEH

    Rezvan, honey, you have the gun with you? Give it back and we'll
       go back to Tehran. I swear to God, I'm about to have a stroke.

Rezvan mulls it over and makes a decision.

65. INT./EXT. THE ORCHARD. MANSION – DAY

While filming Rezvan, Iman follows her to the spot where the car
is parked. Sana and Najmeh are looking at them through the
window. Sana runs towards the door. The door is locked, and it
is not possible to leave.

Rezvan and Iman arrive at the parking spot, near the entrance of
the orchard. Iman opens the car's door with the remote. He takes
out his weapon from behind his back. He prepares it to shoot.
Rezvan opens the door and sits in the back seat. She puts her
hand in the seat cover pocket. But she can't find the gun.
Rezvan is desperate.

                                IMAN

                            what happened?

Rezvan takes out her hand.

                               REZVAN

           I'd put it here, but it is not there anymore.

                                IMAN

                           You're all liars.

The sound of breaking glass can be heard. Iman notices Sana's
possible escape. He hastily grabs Rezvan's hand and drags her
behind him.

                    IMAN

              Come on, run...

They run through the trees towards the mansion. They reach the
mansion. The glass is broken, and Sana is gone.

66. INT. MANSION- DAY

Iman has imprisoned Rezvan and Najmeh in different rooms.

67. EXT. ORCHARD- DAY

Iman replaces the broken glass with a linoleum tablecloth.

Iman searches outside the mansion to find Sana.

Iman is quietly looking for Sana in the orchard.

68. INT. MANSION- DAY

Iman opens a can and pours it in two plates. He fills two
glasses with water. Putting them in a tray, he goes to Rezvan's
and Najmeh's rooms. He unlocks the door of Rezvan's room and
leaves water and food for her. He then opens the door of
Najmeh's room.

                    NAJMEH

              Iman, where is Sana?

Iman doesn't respond.

                    NAJMEH

In a few hours, the weather gets cold, the child will get sick.
   The night here is not safe, there are wild animals out there.
                    Let's go find her.

Iman leaves the food and water without any reaction, locks the
door, and leaves. Najmeh knocks on the door and repeats her
request.

NAJMEH

Iman, what's wrong with you? Open the door, Iman, we are your family.

69. EXT. ORCHARD. SANA'S HIDING PLACE- DAY

Sana is sitting alert and ready in her hiding place, holding the gun in her hand.

70. EXT. MANSION'S PORCH- DAY (ALMOST NIGHT)

While drinking tea, Iman is watching the dried trees of the orchard through the window.

71. INT./EXT. MANSION. ORCHARD- NIGHT

Mansion.

Sitting by the Korsi, Iman reads the prayer book. The sound of knocking on the door and Rezvan's screams that she needs to go to the bathroom can be heard. Iman doesn't pay attention to Rezvan's request for a long time, but finally gets up and goes to the room where Rezvan is imprisoned. He opens the door.

IMAN

When you need something, you knock on the door twice and I will come to in a few minutes. From now on, if you knock hard on the door and shout, I will not come. Get out.

Rezvan comes out of the room furious and enraged. Rezvan walks ahead and Iman walks behind her. They haven't walked more than a few steps when the power goes out.

IMAN

Go back to the room.

REZVAN

I have to go to the bathroom.

                              IMAN

     Hold on a few more minutes, I need to connect the power.

Iman imprisons Rezvan in the room again.

Orchard.

Iman cautiously comes out of the mansion and locks the door. He goes toward the power box. After walking in the orchard for a while, he reaches the power box and reset the fuse.

Mansion.

Iman enters the mansion. He notices that the tablecloth over the broken window is undone. Suddenly he remembers something. He goes toward his bag. The bag with the phones has fallen out and Sana's phone is missing. Iman immediately takes his phone and dials Sana's number. The phone is on, but Sana does not answer. Rezvan knocks on the door again and shouts. Iman looks towards her room. Disregarding Rezvan's screams, he sits there on a chair.

72. EXT. THE ORCHARD. SHED. NEAR THE MANSION- NIGHT

The orchard.

The light of the full moon shines on the orchard. After settling in a proper place, Sana takes out her phone and struggles to find a spot in which she has Internet access. She ignores the messages that have been sent to her in the past two days and starts searching online. In her search, she manages to find the model of the gun. By watching a video, she learns how to work with it. Afterward, quietly, and cautiously, she approaches the mansion.

Near the mansion.

Sana observes the mansion for a while. She approaches the window and carefully tries to see inside the house. Sitting around the Korsi, Iman is reading the prayer book. Sana starts walking toward the orchard's shed among the trees. After a while, she reaches the shed which is on the other side of the orchard.

The shed.

Sana quietly opens the door by untying a piece of wire that has been used instead of a lock and enters. In the dusty storage, next to the gardening tools, there is some mourning equipment, such as Alam, Kottal, a cauldron, and some clothes. In a box, there are several photo frames, including an old family photo in Imam Reza's shrine which draws Sana's attention. Sana looks at the picture for a moment. She stares at his father, who is a five-year-old child with his hand on his chest. She puts the frame aside and continues to check the rest of the items in the shed. She sees a record player and some old cassette tapes wrapped in a plastic bag, looking perfectly intact. she tries one or two cassettes in the audio player; they are Noha and religious speeches. She suddenly notices a microphone and several speakers. A dusty old amplifier with several large speakers, lots of wires, and an old record player gives her the spark of an idea. With curiosity and the help of online searches, Sana learns how to use them. In a box, she collects some tools that she thinks she needs to break the rooms' locks. Then she returns to the mansion with due caution.

near the mansion.

Sana hides the box of tools she collected somewhere near the mansion's door. She looks inside through a hidden window. Iman has put the book aside and is getting ready to sleep. Sana watches him for a while to make sure he is sleeping.

The shed.

Sana returns to the shed. Around midnight, she secretly brings out the speakers from the shed and places them in different spots among the trees facing the mansion. With the necessary wirings, she connects the speakers to the amplifier in the shed. she connects the microphone. While playing a video of his father that she has on the memory of her phone (the picnic by the sea that we have already seen on the video camera), she places the phone in front of the microphone. The sound of this video, which is Iman's affectionate conversation with Sana and Rezvan, spreads throughout the orchard.

73. INT./EXT. MANSION. ORCHARD. THE SHED- NIGHT

Mansion.

Iman is surprised to hear his own voice from speakers in the orchard. He dwells on it for a while. Then he hurriedly opens the door of the mansion and starts running among the trees.

Orchard.

Iman wants to find out where the voice is coming from. But the sound is coming from every corner he turns to. He starts shouting.

> IMAN
>
> Sana...

The shed.

Hearing his shouts, Sana removes the phone and instead, she plays one of the cassette tapes she found using the old cassette player. The sound of Noha echoes in the orchard.

Orchard.

Iman is angry about this game. Seeing the light of the shed, he runs towards it.

The shed.

Sana comes out of the shed and hides in a corner. Iman reaches the shed. He immediately enters and turns off the player. Sana uses this opportunity to close the shed's door and inserts a small iron rod that she prepared in advance into the lock. Iman is now trapped in the shed. He bangs angrily on the door.

> IMAN
>
> Open the door Sana...open the door!

Sana runs towards the mansion. She counts the seconds while running. She then picks up the box she's hidden in advance and takes it with her inside the mansion.

Mansion.

Sana goes toward the room where Rezvan is imprisoned. She takes a hammer from the box.

SANA

I'm here.

NAJMEH

Sana, my darling, are you okay?

SANA

Yes, I'm fine, Mom.

NAJMEH

What are you doing?

SANA

I'm getting you out.

REZVAN

Where is Dad?

SANA

In the tools shed.

Amid the hammer blows, Iman's voice is heard from the speakers.

IMAN

Sana, what are you doing? Come on, open the door, you're making everything worse than it was... don't make me angrier... Sana... Sana!

Indifferent to Iman's voice, Sana continues to bang on the lock.

SANA

If he can open the door, at best it will take him twenty-three seconds to get here.

The lock on the door of Rezvan's room breaks. Rezvan comes out and they hug each other. Both go toward their mother's room. They try to open the door by using a hammer to break the lock.

REZVAN

Dad's voice stopped.

                         SANA

                         Count.

Sana counts the seconds with every blow. following her, Rezvan
counts, and then Najmeh.

the shed.

The iron rod in the lock is moving as Iman bangs on the door and
now it's on the verge of coming out of its place.

Mansion.

After a few more knocks, the door of Najmeh's room opens. Najmeh
comes out and hugs the children. Sana shouts.

                         SANA

                       let's go...

Reaching the kitchen, Rezvan looks for the car keys, but it's
nowhere to be found.

                         SANA

  Come on, don't waste time, we don't need a car... he's gonna be
                     here any minute now.

Orchard.

Najmeh and the girls go toward the entrance through the
orchard's trees.

74. EXT. DESERT. ABANDONED VILLAGE- NIGHT

In the open shot under the moonlight, Najmeh, Rezvan, and Sana
are running in the desert towards the abandoned village.
Suddenly, two points of light (Iman's car) come toward them from
the orchard. Near the village, Rezvan notices Iman's car. She
shouts.

                        REZVAN

              Run in different directions!

Najmeh, Rezvan, and Sana enter the ruins of the village, each in a different direction.

After a few moments, Iman's car stops in front of the village amidst the dust raised by the tires. He gets out of the car and enters the village. Iman is searching for Sana, Rezvan, and Najmeh.

Rezvan, Sana, and Najmeh are searching for a shelter to stay out of Iman's sight.

75. EXT. ABANDONED VILLAGE- DAWN TO SUNRISE (SUN RISES AND LIGHTS UP THE SKY DURING THIS SCENE)

After searching for a while, Iman hears a voice from the roof of the room he is in. He quietly climbs up the roof from the worn-out brick walls and fragile stairs. Najmeh has taken refuge in a corner. Iman traps her from behind.

IMAN

Don't move.

Najmeh turns towards Iman.

NAJMEH
I'll move. what do you want to do? Is there anything left that you haven't done already?
You just didn't shoot...shoot then.

IMAN

Be quiet, don't speak, sit down.

NAJMEH

I'll speak, we won't sit.

Najmeh doesn't sit. She is looking at Iman. Suddenly she shouts.

NAJMEH

He's here girls.

Iman smacks Najmeh right in the mouth.

IMAN

>   I'm telling you to sit down.

Najmeh wipes her mouth.

                              NAJMEH

                            I won't.

Iman suddenly attacks her and grabs her hair in his fist. Najmeh falls on the ground and screams. The sound of Najmeh's screams attracts Sana's attention. Sana runs toward the sound. She sees this scene from a distance: Iman is pulling Najmeh by the hair and drags her on the ground. Sana is enraged by seeing this scene. She quickly brings herself to a spot to surprise Iman. She stands behind a wall and waits. As soon as Iman approaches, she comes out of the ambush and points the gun at her father.

                              SANA

                        Enough! Stop this.

Iman stops. He pretends to be happy to see Sana.

                              IMAN

                       So you finally show up…

                              SANA

                       Let her go, get up, Mom.

Najmeh has fallen at Iman's feet.

                              NAJMEH

  For the love of God, let it go, Iman. Don't hurt the children,
                  you destroyed everything, but why?

Iman ignores Najmeh's pleas and speaks to Sana in a contemptuous tone.

                              IMAN

                           can you shoot?

                              SANA

                         yes, I know how to.

IMAN

Where did you learn?

SANA

Don't, Dad, stay right there. Otherwise, I swear I'll shoot you... I'm very angry.

IMAN

Shoot your dad?

SANA

Yes, seeing the things you've done, I can shoot you easily.

IMAN

Do it then.

NAJMEH

Sana, dear, your dad is not well. Give him the gun and everything will end here.

Sana is staring at Iman. Iman releases Najmeh's hair and little by little, approaches Sana very slowly.

SANA

It doesn't end, mom, nothing's going to end. Everything has been like this ever since I can remember. You've always surrendered and gave him whatever he wanted.
It's the same now, even if he takes the gun, it won't end.

Iman continues to gradually approach Sana. Sana is staring at him in the eyes. None of them realize that the roof surface is fragile and unreliable. Sana shouts.

SANA

Dad, I swear to God, I'll shoot you, don't...

Iman comes forward. Sana goes back. Rezvan arrives right from behind Iman. She sits on the floor next to Najmeh. Sana shouts.

SANA

Rezvan, tell him to stop.

Iman doesn't pay attention.

                    REZVAN

          Sana, let him go, let's leave.

Suddenly, taking advantage of the opportunity, Iman charges toward Sana to surprise her. Sana pulls the trigger with a spontaneous scream. The bullet hits the fragile roof, and it collapses. Iman is thrown from the roof to the lower floor on a pile of dirt. A cloud of heavy dust rises. The weakness of the building causes more debris to fall on top of each other. Najmeh is shouting.Among the rubbles, the gun can be seen in Iman's hand.

The image cuts to documentary videos (recorded with mobile phones), showing scenes of protests and the shout of brave young women, evoking resistance and hope for freedom.

Printed in Great Britain
by Amazon